THERE IS
NO GOOD CARD
FOR THIS

THERE IS NO GOOD CARD FOR THIS

WHAT to SAY and DO WHEN LIFE is SCARY, AWFUL, and UNFAIR to PEOPLE You LOVE

Kelsey Crowe, Ph.D.,
and Emily McDowell

HarperOne
An Imprint of HarperCollins Publishers

Some names have been changed in this book to protect people's privacy.

HarperCollins books may be purchased for educational, business, or sales promotional use. For information, please email the Special Markets Department at SPsales@harpercollins.com.

FIRST EDITION

Designed by Ad Librum

Library of Congress Cataloging-in-Publication Data
Names: Crowe, Kelsey, author. | McDowell, Emily, author.
Title: There is no good card for this : what to say and do when life is scary, awful, and unfair to people you love / Dr. Kelsey Crowe, Emily McDowell.
Description: San Francisco : HarperOne, 2017.
Identifiers: LCCN 2016028082 (print) | LCCN 2016048367 (ebook) |
ISBN 9780062469991 (hardback) | ISBN 9780062658579 (audio) |
ISBN 9780062470003 (e-book)
Subjects: LCSH: Self-actualization (Psychology) | Bereavement. | Loss (Psychology) |
BISAC: SELF-HELP / Personal Growth / General. |
FAMILY & RELATIONSHIPS / Death, Grief, Bereavement.
Classification: LCC BF637.S4 C769 2017 (print) | LCC BF637.S4 (ebook) |
DDC 155.9/3—dc23
LC record available at https://lccn.loc.gov/2016028082

17 18 19 20 21 LSC/C 10 9 8 7 6 5 4 3

THERE *is* NOTHING
I WOULD NOT DO
FOR THOSE WHO ARE
REALLY MY FRIENDS.
I HAVE NO NOTION OF
LOVING PEOPLE BY HALVES;
IT IS NOT MY NATURE.

— JANE AUSTEN —
NORTHANGER ABBEY

UHH... WOW.
LET ME KNOW IF THERE'S
ANYTHING I CAN DO?

— MOST OF US —
MOST OF THE TIME

CONTENTS

Introduction   Life Spoiler Alert: Bad Things Happen   1

PART ONE: LAYING SOME GROUNDWORK

Chapter 1   Put Your Own Oxygen Mask on First   19
Chapter 2   Standing in Their Shoes   43

PART TWO: The THREE TOUCHSTONES of SHOWING UP

Chapter 3   Your Kindness Is Your Credential   55
Chapter 4   Listening Speaks Volumes   87
Chapter 5   Small Gestures Make a Big Difference   143

PART THREE: JUST HELP ME NOT BE A DISASTER

Chapter 6   Please Never Say This (Thanks!)   185
Chapter 7   Empathy Directory:
                 Dos and Don'ts Cheat Sheets   227
Conclusion   You Got This!   241

References   245
About the Research   249
Acknowledgments   253
About the Authors   259

INTRODUCTION

LIFE *Spoiler* ALERT: BAD THINGS HAPPEN

To begin, we present to you a true story about trying to console a friend in a tough situation, which shows how our best intentions can go off the rails fast.

Monique and Amy were out for a run one morning. As the two friends ran slowly up a hill, Monique chatted idly about herself: "What should I do this weekend? Maybe a movie . . . though I need a haircut. Something short? Should I get bangs again?"

Then Amy slowed to a stop.

"Monique," Amy said, "I was diagnosed with breast cancer yesterday."

Monique's mouth went dry. *What do I say?* "I'm so sorry," she said. "That must be so horrible for you." Monique hugged her and quickly pulled away. Monique asked for more details, and as they talked, the initial shock wore off a bit. And then Monique said:

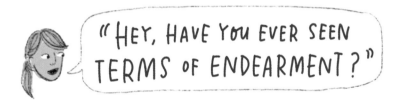

The two friends were at the bottom of the hill now. They stopped again, and Amy, as if catching her breath, stared at her incredulously.

"The movie?"

"Yeah," Monique said. "With Debra Winger."

"Right. And she's a . . . young mother? Who dies of breast cancer?"

"Oh." Monique's mind tumbled and turned. She *was* talking about that movie, but she'd meant to reference another part—a funny part. Humor was always Monique's first resort for everything, including being scared.

BuT Monique HAD FoRGOTTEN a KIND oF IMPORTANT DETAIL: DEBRA WINGER DIED AT THE END oF THE MOVIE.

"Never mind!" Monique said. "Just kidding."

"Wait. I just told you that I have cancer, and now you want me to watch the saddest movie of all time about someone who dies of cancer?"

"I'm a dumbass," Monique said.

"Yes," Amy said. "Yes, you are."

We've all been there, haven't we?

The phone rings, and someone you love is sobbing. Your gut tightens, your pulse quickens. A coworker's child has been born with a serious heart condition, or someone's husband has been in a car accident, or a friend has been diagnosed with a terminal illness.

WHATEVER *it* IS,

a PERSON'S LIFE *has* JUST FALLEN APART, *and* YOU FEEL AWFUL, *and* YOU ALSO HAVE NO FREAKING CLUE WHAT *to* SAY,

LET ALONE DO.

Well, there's a reason you don't know what to say. In some situations, there are absolutely no words that will make things better. There's nobody on earth who can make everything okay for a mother who has lost her child, or for a man whose wife was diagnosed with cancer. That's one reason many of us say nothing at all.

The bad news is that you're right—you probably aren't going to fix anyone's pain with your words. But the good news is that no human being can, so there's nothing wrong with you if you can't come up with the Perfect Thing to Say.

> *"I genuinely think that anything anyone said to me,*
> *whenever they said it, was okay. Some things helped*
> *more than others, but anyone who had the courage*
> *to reach out and speak to me made me feel better."*
>
> —Anne, who lost her mother

And *doing* something to help? Well, that's even better. Figuring out what to do may sound harder than knowing what to say, but by the end of this book you will know how to do both. And it won't be hard. You'll simply learn all the ways in which you're already good at being a friend, and we'll help you with the rest.

WHISKEY for the WOUNDED

This book is not chicken soup for the soul; it's whiskey for the wounded. So don't expect a self-help, miracle-making volume on how to "transform" you into the world's most empathetic person. We will also assume that because you graduated from kinder-garten, you already know that empathy and compas-sion are important, and that being a helpful friend is a good way to be. Another assumption we'll take the liberty of stating right now: you are not perfect, and we don't

BECOMING DR. OPRAH GANDHI

NOPE.

expect you to become perfect at this, because there's no such thing anyway. We are not trying to make you a Textbook Gold Star Helper, creating yet another (impossible) goal.

The first time something unimaginably terrible happens to a friend—and it *will* happen at some point—you may get a pass for awkward behavior. Yet as time goes on, if you want to be a responsible grown-up, you've got to do a little better than that. When someone in your life is hurting, there are real, concrete ways to help. And that's what we're here for.

We know, however, that there are definitely times to *not* reach out, to *not* say anything—we can't all show up at every bad turn in someone's life. And equally true: not everyone wants you to be involved in their particular difficult situation. It's not our intention to turn you into an overbearing do-gooder. Our goal is to help you get a basic foundation in giving comfort, assess the difference between being supportive and being a buttinsky, and ultimately, to help you move past just *thinking* about a suffering person, to actually *doing* something (even a small thing) if the situation calls for it, and doing it with confidence instead of fear of what could go wrong.

There are a few different ways to use this book. No doubt, many of you have a friend in crisis right now, and if that's the case, you're probably looking for some handy, practical things to say and do that will help today. You'll find those in Parts 2 and 3. In fact, if you have only four minutes in which to figure out what to say to your grieving colleague, Part 3 has got you covered. For those who are ready, however, Part 1 gets at the hows and whys of our struggle to connect in times of suffering. It offers ways to reflect on (and put down) our own psychological baggage and fears, which are often what get in the way of reaching out at all.

Taking the time to work on your mind-set as well as the skills we offer in this book will make your life *easier*, not harder. That might seem counterintuitive, since reaching out means adding one more to-do item in your already busy schedule. But you'll find that making the effort to connect is worth the peace of mind it brings—not to mention a better night's sleep, because you aren't lying awake at night feeling like a terrible person for not emailing so-and-so.

In addition to the feeling of well-being that comes with aligning your actions with your intentions, this empathy practice will result in more meaningful connections. Not just in terms of what you give, but in terms of what you receive. Your circle of care will widen, from your best friend to a colleague to a neighbor to a casual acquaintance to even a stranger. It sounds paradoxical, but it's true: being there in moments of suffering can actually lead to more joy.

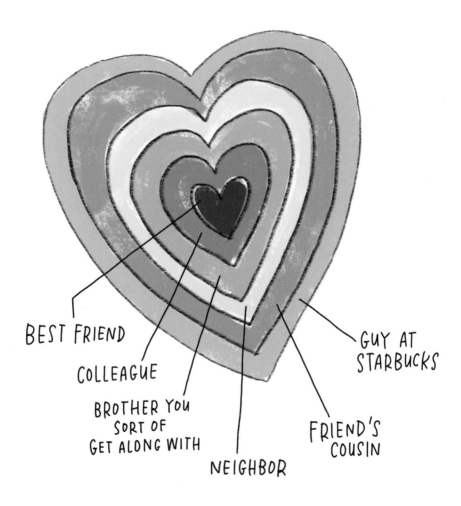

BEST FRIEND

COLLEAGUE

BROTHER YOU
SORT OF
GET ALONG WITH

NEIGHBOR

FRIEND'S
COUSIN

GUY AT
STARBUCKS

WHY LISTEN to US?

We are people. Like many of you, we've had our ups and downs in life, and as a result, we both ended up fascinated by this topic, but in completely different ways. It's safe to say that our early twenties pretty much sucked, though for different reasons.

KELSEY'S Story:

I had lost my mother to mental illness when I was twenty-one years old. She was my only parent. I had no siblings, aunts, or uncles, and my grandparents had long since passed away. Despite her illness, my mother and I were always incredibly close; and then, she decided to stop taking psychotropic medication. The result was paranoia and delusions that became all consuming. After I tried getting her into a hospital for help, she never spoke to me again; and a few years later, she died. When my mother rejected me, my tiny, but entire family was gone. It was a loss that comes with no ritual for mourning— where, save my closest friends, the "death" of the dearest person in my life was basically unmentioned.

EMILY'S Story:

When I was twenty-four years old, I was diagnosed with stage 3 Hodgkin's lymphoma. After nine months of chemo and radiation, I went into remission and have been cancer free for fifteen years (knock on wood!). The most difficult part of my illness wasn't losing my hair, or being erroneously called "sir" by Starbucks baristas, or sickness from chemo. It was the loneliness and isolation I felt when many of my close friends and family members disappeared because they didn't know what to say or said the absolute wrong thing without realizing it.

And, for both of us, with age came more challenging stuff (as is normal for us humans). Cancer showed up again: Emily lost her college roommate and her father-in-law to it, and Kelsey was treated for breast cancer, twice. Our experiences alone didn't make us empathy experts—they just made us understand how important it is, in difficult times, to have support from the people in our lives.

But without clear instructions about what to do or say, it can be easy to doubt your own capacity to provide support. And with an absence of social ritual or models about how to support someone in a really difficult time, we may not recognize that doing or saying something—anything—could be a really big deal for someone who is scared or grieving.

With all that in mind, we have both worked in our individual ways to make it a little easier for people to show up when life is hard.

EMILY USED HER PLATFORM as a GREETING CARD WRITER and ILLUSTRATOR, her experience as a cancer survivor, and the lessons she learned around the loss of her close college friend to launch her line of Empathy Cards, specifically designed to give us more authentic ways of connecting around illness and grief. KELSEY FOUNDED an ORGANIZATION CALLED HELP EACH OTHER OUT, which provides Empathy Bootcamps, workshops on Being There for people we care about, developed with input from empathy experts and advisers from the fields of business, medicine, and grief counseling. To inform these workshops, and to write this book, she also did extensive online survey research with over nine hundred people, and interviewed fifty other people who had been through all kinds of difficult times, all to learn what support worked, and what didn't.

What Kelsey learned from her research and from Empathy Bootcamps offered in university, hospital, and business settings, and what Emily found in the incredible response to her Empathy Cards, is this:

WHETHER YOU'RE A PROFESSIONAL SOCIAL WORKER OR A FREAKED-OUT BEST FRIEND, IF YOU'RE STRUGGLING WITH HOW to SUPPORT SOMEONE WHO IS HURTING, YOU ARE NOT ALONE.

This is something virtually everyone wrestles with at some point. Both of us definitely have.

All our research and engagement around grief has enhanced, and considerably changed, our own previously held beliefs about what is and isn't supportive. We want to spare you from making the same mistakes we've made and offer you what we've learned in a straightforward, we've-all-been-that-dumbass kind of way.

OUR APPROACH

Our approach boils down to one word: *trust*. When it comes to supporting the people you care about, trusting yourself— your ability to be kind and care, your values, and what you can authentically do—is the key to navigating life's worst neighborhoods.

To help you learn to trust yourself in this arena, we dive into three credos in this book that we call:

THE THREE TOUCHSTONES OF SHOWING UP:

1) YOUR KINDNESS IS YOUR CREDENTIAL.

2) LISTENING SPEAKS VOLUMES.

3) SMALL GESTURES MAKE A BIG DIFFERENCE.

By exploring the meaning as well as the practical application of these touchstones in your life, you will feel more confident to give.

If you think an awkward response to a friend's crisis will make them feel bad, then you should know that if you say nothing, they will likely feel worse. But don't worry: you're not on your own. This book will empower you with the confidence to reach out to others—friends, family, acquaintances, and even strangers—in their difficult times, fostering everlasting (or momentary) deep connections. We will help move you past the analysis paralysis of just *thinking* about a person who's having a hard time to actually *doing* something for that person, and doing it with good judgment.

IF YOU TAKE ONE THING AWAY FROM THIS BOOK, IT SHOULD BE THIS:

IF YOU'RE CHOOSING BETWEEN SAYING SOMETHING AND SAYING NOTHING, YOU'RE ALMOST ALWAYS BETTER OFF SAYING SOMETHING.

And when someone in your life is hurting, there are real, concrete ways to help. CHANCES ARE, YOU'VE PROBABLY GOT A FRIEND IN NEED AT THIS VERY MOMENT.

PART ONE:

Laying SOME

GROUNDWORK

CHAPTER 1:
PUT YOUR OWN OXYGEN MASK on FIRST

"I think people don't ask or say anything because
it's an uncomfortable topic. In the meantime, I'm
going through a huge life transition and it's like the
elephant in the room that is not being addressed.
I think that's the main thing—that most people just
don't ask or don't say anything."

—Carla, divorced

It goes like this: A work colleague loses his spouse, and you, who have never experienced a loss like this, don't know what to do to help. (Hell, you never even knew he *had* a spouse.) For his part, well, he's always been supersupportive when you faced a tough deadline, and he's always just the right amount of office-friendly. You've shared pictures of your cats doing weird things. You definitely care about each other, but you aren't close friends.

SO YOU DO WHAT many OF US DO iN THIS KIND OF SITUATION:

you TOTALLY AVOID the BEREAVED MAN'S GAZE at EVERY TURN.

But it's not as if you're an uncaring person, so you wait patiently for the *exact* right words to come to you. *And they will come*, you tell yourself. Weeks go by, and they never do. And now, you're skipping your coffee breaks to avoid running into your colleague at the vending machine, and every time you see him, you feel like a terrible person, and you also really miss coffee.

It happens to us all—a flash of goodwill when something bad happens to people fades into a deep-seated regret, and even shame. But it's probably better this way, right? You don't want to upset him—best to play it safe. But deep down, safe feels like a cop-out.

If you're somebody who'd rather take the long way back to your desk to spare yourself an awkward encounter with the bereaved . . . take heart, because we have *all* been there. How do we move from uncomfortable avoidance to actually saying or doing something helpful?

We start by first trusting that we are capable of reaching out.

And that means looking at what makes us so insecure about reaching out in the first place. We have a few ideas, which we're serving up as short exercises below. These exercises take just a little time and preparation to do, and they address some common hang-ups about reaching out that we develop over our lifetimes. Get out some stickies, a writing pad, or journal, and feel free to see if a friend or two are game to do this with you. Or just read along "as if," giving yourself time to pause and reflect on the questions.

EMPATHY WARM-UP:
WHAT'S your ROADBLOCK?

Think about an instance when you shied away from someone in a difficult time—a good friend, colleague, neighbor, family member, anyone. We're not talking about someone who pushed your boundaries and drained all your empathy fuel. We're talking about the person you *wanted* to reach out to, but didn't. And importantly, not because *they* thought you should, but because *you* thought you should.

Now, think about your reasons for *not* reaching out. If you're alone, feel free to write them down on a piece of paper. If you're with a friend, write them down, and then use a few minutes to each share your stories of shying away. (You may be surprised to discover just how long this conversation can be.)

When reflecting on your reasons for shying away and feeling like you let yourself and/or your loved ones down, here is something to remember: we all carry regrets. In her Empathy Bootcamps, Kelsey has collected hundreds of people's regrets about shying away. Here are just a few:

I WISH I'D CALLED MY FRIEND in the PAST YEAR SINCE HER FATHER DIED.

I FEEL I HAVEN'T BEEN THERE ENOUGH FOR MY NIECE and NEPHEWS WHOSE MOM DIED, EVEN THOUGH I WORK in THE DEATH and DYING FIELD.

I REGRET SHYING AWAY FROM a CHURCH FRIEND WHO WAS DYING OF CANCER. I WAS SCARED.

I'M SORRY, SUE. I WASN'T THERE FOR YOU in LONDON. I WAS AFRAID. I'M WITH YOU NOW.

I WISH I'D VISITED MY UNCLE in THE HOSPITAL.

I'M SORRY, MOM. I DIDN'T UNDERSTAND YOUR PAIN. I WAS SO LITTLE.

I WISH I'D REACHED OUT to MY FRIEND AFTER HER MISCARRIAGE. I DIDN'T KNOW WHAT to SAY.

THREE
EMPATHY ROADBLOCKS:

What makes us shy away? Meet the Empathy Roadblocks:

- ## FEAR OF DOING THE WRONG THING

  "Oh God, what if I make it worse?" We feel pressure to cure the situation with the perfect gesture, and if we fail, we fear we'll ruin a relationship, or just embarrass ourselves.

- ## FEAR OF SAYING THE WRONG THING

  We don't know if we are supposed to know certain things; we don't want to make someone feel like the source of gossip; we don't want to bring up negative feelings if someone wasn't thinking about that awful thing that happened. If we're not really close to the person (e.g., a coworker), we might feel like it's not our "place" to help, and that when we do, we'll say something that makes them feel worse.

- ## FEAR OF NOT HAVING TIME/BANDWIDTH

  We're busy, life is crazy, and we don't want to commit to more than we can handle. We're not sure how much of a commitment this stuff involves.

GOOD NEWS:
WE'RE making IT HARDER THAN IT NEEDS to BE!

One day, while in the car on the way to preschool, Kelsey's young daughter Georgia piped up from the backseat, "Mom, what do you actually do for a living?" Kelsey paused, trying to come up with an answer.

"Well," Kelsey said, "I help friends be there for each other when they are sad."

"Oh," said Georgia, "that's *easy*."

"Oh, *really*?" said Kelsey. "What would you say to help someone in need?"

Then Georgia rattled off this list:

- I'M SORRY.
- DO you WANT to PLAY WITH ME?
- DO you WANT to TAKE A LITTLE BREAK?
- DO YOU WANT a LITTLE HUG?

Take a minute and read this short list again, and consider that Georgia just blew up the notion that helping isn't an ability we're born with, or a skill we naturally pick up between learning to tie our shoes and figuring out a glue stick. Sadly, something happens as we grow up. We change from being completely unself-conscious and intuitive about how to comfort someone to being self-doubting, freaked-out messes.

How did we get here? We believe it comes down to what Aaron T. Beck—widely considered the founder of cognitive psychology—describes as our two main fears:

1. I am unlovable.
2. I am incompetent.

That about covers it, doesn't it?

We've all felt the emotional sting when our overtures of friendship are rejected, our intentions are misunderstood, or our attempts at being kind are disregarded. These little hurts start on the playground and build up over a lifetime. We've all had the feeling of being unable to connect and, buried deep below that, considered the Universal Questions that gnaw at us:

And, as we all know, doubts like these remind us of our limitations. So, often we try and play it safe by avoiding the situation altogether. When someone is in a difficult time that we don't understand, the stakes can feel pretty high. And it's really, really tempting to avoid the risk of failure entirely, especially when we are not sure if trying will help.

But here's the thing: you can pretend to be somebody who doesn't make mistakes, but (a) that's impossible, and (b) it's not actually all that supportive. Because when we're feeling vulnerable and scared, who do we immediately want to turn to? It probably *isn't* the person we know whose life appears to be perfect. We go to the person we trust. And this has very little to do with perfection. (Often, it's the opposite.)

If we really want to have authentic connections with others, then we need to talk about two kinds of psychological baggage we tend to carry around, which make us completely self-conscious about our capacity to connect with people: (1) guilt about how we've let others down, and (2) resentment about being let down by others in the past. The resulting beliefs—that we are not enough, and that others are not enough—get in the way of trusting our innate capacities to give.

EMPATHY WARM-UP:
You're Good Enough,
You're Smart Enough,
You Know the Rest.

You've been let down—we all have—but you've let someone down, too, and because we're not monsters, we feel guilty about that. Guilt can be useful when it reminds us to do better, and when it lifts us up to be more responsible, mature people. But when guilt's end game is simply more guilt with a side of guilt, without ever changing us for the better, then it only drags us down.

One way to free ourselves of guilt is simply to accept who we are. (There's a good reason the Internet is plastered with quotes about this.) Kelsey can feel guilty every time she gets a scone with her morning coffee. Or she can accept that she likes (needs) a deliciously carby reward for making it out of bed and grooming herself most mornings, and that with middle age fast approaching, her college body is a thing of the past. It feels really grown-up in a good way when we accept things about ourselves, like not wearing heels, not liking whiskey, or not wanting to tell the cabdriver our life story on the way to the airport. Then we can relax into who we really are and stop using up energy on things that don't matter.

I WILL NEVER DRINK ENOUGH WATER!
I WEAR THE SAME PANTS a LOT!
I DON'T CARE ABOUT WINE!
I TOTALLY DON'T GET SUSHI!
I ACCEPT MYSELF!
I THINK DOGS ARE ANNOYING!
I LOVE SHOWS ABOUT MAKEOVERS!
I NEED NINE HOURS OF SLEEP!
YOGA BORES ME!
I EAT FROZEN PIZZA BY CHOICE!

Some of the ways we manage guilt, however, are not so helpful. Particularly: avoiding guilt by resigning ourselves to being less than we are—meaning less capable, less loving, less present. It's a self-defeating, rather than self-actualized, choice. For example, it's one thing for Kelsey to accept that a scone is a small price to pay for a good mood in the morning. It's quite another to tell ourselves that people are better off without our help because we're just no good at giving it. Not only is that not true—it's a lot easier to learn to be kind than it is to give up carbs—but it's also dangerous.

BELIEVING THAT you're INCAPABLE OF CONNECTING DURING PAINFUL TIMES CAN ISOLATE you FROM LIFE'S MOST CONNECTED MOMENTS.

In this book, we'll give you a lot of really helpful tips on showing up that even the most feelings-averse among us can master. But to believe that these skills will work, you will first need to believe in the benefit of you, THE FLAWED YOU, trying. And that begins with being *a lot* less hard on yourself.

So we're going to ask that you get some of that guilt off your chest.

EMPATHY WORKOUT:
BEING KIND to OTHERS
BEGINS WITH BEING KIND to OURSELVES.

- Take some stickie notes or index cards, or cut some paper to create your own cards, and write down one to three times when you shied away from someone's suffering. Consider the following truths (yes, they are true):
  - Because I shied away, it does not make me an awful person.
  - Because I shied away, it does not mean I am bad at empathy.

- Write out your regret on the cards: "I regret _____." Consider this as you fill the cards out: "I did the best I could with the tools I had at the time." Because that's probably true, too.

- You also have permission to admit some of the deeper things that got in the way of reaching out. Like the following:
  - I was self-involved and didn't see their suffering.
  - I didn't think my effort would matter that much.
  - I was afraid of getting sucked in.
  - I was afraid I wouldn't be able to give enough.

- And then write out on your cards: "I forgive myself for a time I shied away because _____."

- Now, take your cards, and create a little ceremony of letting them go. You could burn them on the beach, in your yard, or in your fireplace—or a sink or trash can will do just fine if you don't have access to a beach, yard, or fireplace. Or plant them in the soil with a seed or young sapling. Or fold them into paper airplanes and send them off the roof of your building. You get the idea.

We've found that actually destroying the paper makes a psychic difference, instead of just throwing it in the garbage or leaving it in a journal. It sounds a little woo-woo, but having your own personal ritual of letting go can literally (and symbolically) feel like the psychological baggage of guilt is burned away.

NEXT UP: SCARY Conversation TIP #1

You can apologize to the person you shied away from, too, if you want to. You can do it with an email or a card, or you can talk. And you know what? It may be that the behavior you've been agonizing over for years is not even remembered by the person you're reaching out to. Or it's possible that reaching out may bring up some anger you will have to accept. Or it may result in sincere appreciation for your intention to make things right.

EMILY Says: *When I got sick, I was twenty-four. If you've ever known a twenty-four-year-old, or been one, you understand that in general, this is not exactly an age rife with sage wisdom and life experience. None of my close friends had ever known anyone with cancer beyond a grandparent, let alone someone their age. Everyone was really scared, and we all fumbled very awkwardly through it. Some people shied away because they didn't know how to handle it, and at the time, I interpreted it as them not caring about me.*

Over the years, various friends have reached out to apologize for things they did or didn't do during that time. In a couple of cases, this was over ten years later. A lot of the time, I didn't even recall the particular thing they'd been lying awake at night over. These conversations have clearly been way more stressful for the other person than for me, and even though I let go of any resentment long ago (if there ever was any to begin with), it's been really touching and meaningful to me every time someone reached out.

LETTING Resentments GO

We're human. Most of us carry grudges. They can be useful, too. Grudges are helpful in shielding us from the people in our lives

who've treated us badly or taken advantage of our vulnerability. But as much as that coping strategy might work to protect us in the short term, too many grudges are like excess scar tissue, blocking our ability to make rewarding emotional connections. That's when our smart strategies at self-preservation turn into harmful forms of self-sabotage. If we want to develop relationships that weather life's imperfect times, we have to be capable of weathering people's imperfections, too.

One way to let go of these resentments that no longer serve us is to first consider what *was* given to us that we may have failed to notice at the time.

IN ORDER to RECEIVE, WE MUST NOTICE WHAT is GIVEN.

In the depths of our suffering, "valuing what we receive" can be a lot harder than it sounds. Sometimes, the vastness and intensity of emotions of despair or fear can crowd everything else out and keep us from seeing the beautiful things being offered to us. The irony, of course, is that this is the time when we need these beautiful things the most.

KELSEY Says:

My own family experience taught me the value of being able to receive care, however I found it. But this lesson didn't come easy. My younger life narrative—the one in which I believed no adult had stepped up when I lost my mother to mental illness—experienced a much needed shift when I happened upon some contradictory evidence.

The evidence was in the form of a letter, which came while I was volunteering with the Peace Corps in Africa. I'd written to my mother's only friend about being scared to return to the United States with no place to go home to. In her response, my mother's friend didn't offer me a place to stay, and that had hurt. Fifteen years later, I read the letter again and found something important that I had failed to see earlier, which represented a completely different story from the one I'd told myself.

My mother's friend had actually written: "Sometimes we all need a mom. I want to be your mom when you need one."

Somehow, in the depths of my longing, I missed what I had probably most needed to hear. And it's probably true that I was disappointed with many of the people in my life, which upon reflection, was a lot about failing to notice what I was being given.

We know this is difficult advice to follow, but when you think about your experience of pain, and how others were or were not there for you, it's useful to pay close attention to, and learn to recognize, who is there for you now. Notice each gesture from a friend, family member, stranger, colleague, or neighbor that comes your way to give you comfort: a hug, a listening ear, a car ride, an offer to see a movie. Cherish it. No need to write a thank-you note or express anything outwardly—just the act of *noticing* the gesture will reflect your gratitude and make you an easier person to whom to give.

This act of noticing and gratitude is not about becoming someone who sees the bright side of everything (because that person is really f'ing annoying). Instead, it's about opening ourselves up to notice the generosity that is actually there, and often, that comes in forms we never expected.

IF WE VIEW PEOPLE'S EFFORTS OF KINDNESS as "NOT ENOUGH," then WE WILL LIKELY CONTINUE to BE DISAPPOINTED.

That's because if people are afraid of failing us, they will more likely shy away. Not because they are bad people or evil people. Like all of us, they're just scared humans who hate the feeling of failure.

There are people who let us down, over and over again, and learning to expect less of them is a great practice in self-care. But the kind of people we want to be attracting in our lives are sincere and well-meaning. With them in mind, we advise that the more likely we are to notice what we do receive, the less likely we are to notice what we failed to get.

This is a useful outlook that helps us not only experience more bounty, but also give with more joy, too. Because when we feel others have failed us with their "deficient" efforts, we'll often judge our own efforts to comfort by the same (impossible) standards. Such high standards of ourselves can make us feel inadequate, prompting us to shy away and do nothing for fear our effort will fall short. Or, they can cause us to give too much or with excessive worry, which are tendencies that make our gifts harder to receive. (We explain what both of these possibilities look like on page 76.)

THE MORE WE CAN APPRECIATE the SMALL GIFTS THAT WE RECEIVE, the MORE WE CAN APPRECIATE THE SMALL GIFTS that WE OFFER.

EMPATHY WORKOUT:
THERE'S MEDICINE in FORGIVENESS.

- Think about someone who let you down in either a big or small way, but in a way that really matters to you— it could be a close friend, a family member, a neighbor, anybody. (Don't think about somebody who *always* lets you down; that person should just be an ex-friend.)

- Write down a small fictional note to that person with this prompt: "I felt let down when you _____."

- But before you write the note, ask yourself these questions. (The answers could be yes to any or all of these, and you still are allowed to feel disappointed. The answer could be no to all of these, and you still are allowed to feel disappointed.)

  — Did I fully admit to my needs at this time?
  — Was I able to fully appreciate the person's authentic gift (that didn't look like what I thought should be offered)?
  — Did I ask for more than this person could handle at this one time, or over a series of times?
  — Is the person a different person now?

- And then: if you feel prepared, you can consider forgiving this person. The point of forgiveness is not for the other person's benefit. It's purely for yours. Because once you recognize your grudge or anger and see its source, this will help bring compassion and empathy to the situation and help you discard the resentment that can get in the way of helping others who need you.

"I forgive the person for shying away from me because

_____."

EMPATHY TIP: Forgiveness doesn't mean burying our feelings and crossing our fingers that they'll just go away. In order to successfully forgive, we need to take a look at the source of our anger or hurt, with the help of listening friends and occasionally, a professional. Often, such feelings are rooted in our own sense of unworthiness. Forgiveness comes when we're able to recognize that the other person's actions were more about them—their own motivations and context—than about us. (And that insight may or may not justify their behavior.) It's not so much that we forgive to forget, but that we forgive in order to learn about others, learn about ourselves, and let go of resentments that hold us down.

NEXT UP: SCARY Conversation TIP #2

Once you've done the above exercise of letting go of resentment, consider how you might talk to the person about how you felt let down. Yikes! Scary. This is a very vulnerable conversation to have, so we'd suggest doing two things:

1. Start by telling your friend you feel really vulnerable even raising this issue.

2. Then tell your friend that you want to build a stronger connection with them by first recognizing a basic fact about humanity:

THIS SHIT IS HARD FOR ANY OF US.

BOTTOM Line:
WE ALL MESS UP
(BECAUSE WE'RE ALL HUMAN)

When looking back at all the cringe-inducing things you might have said or done to someone in their darkest hour, it's easy to feel like you don't have the right kind of fancy emotional training to provide support. And when thinking back on the times when we have been let down by others, we may feel ashamed of how needy we were, that we didn't deserve support, or maybe that we weren't lovable enough to be supported.

Just because most of us aren't confident about knowing what to do, or because we have some baggage about being let down or letting others down, that doesn't mean we're all fatally flawed in the empathy department—it just means we're human. And humans get scared, awkward, and uncomfortable.

Now that we've unpacked some of our own fears and issues around showing up, let's take a look from the other side: the perspective of the person in crisis.

THE FIVE STAGES OF GRIEF:

CRYING IN PUBLIC

CRYING IN THE CAR

CRYING ALONE WHILE
WATCHING TV

CRYING AT WORK

CRYING WHEN YOU'RE
A LITTLE DRUNK

I LOVE YOU.

CHAPTER 2:
STANDING in THEIR SHOES

"Friends and family turned away when we needed them most."
  —Mary, whose toddler was diagnosed with leukemia

Alexandra looked at the "Five Stages of Grief" poster in her therapist's office and wanted to scream, laugh, and cry at the same time. *Five stages?* she thought. *How about five hundred.*

Her sister had died in a car accident six months earlier. Alexandra had gone back to work a week later, since she couldn't afford not to, and that's just what people do. There had been a recognized mourning period, where it felt permissible for her to be sad, but that had long since passed, and everyone around her seemed to just be back to normal. Back to spreadsheets, and pointless meetings about sales targets, and stupid things like fighting with strangers over parking spaces.

But Alexandra wasn't back to normal; there was no normal to go back to. There was just this new reality in which everything she did felt inappropriate: she was fine one minute, then crying uncontrollably as a sudden wave of grief hit her. (Bonus points if it happened in a really public place, like the fruit section of the grocery store.) She didn't know how to relate to anyone, and she didn't know how to talk about it. When friends called, she could hardly stand to hear her own bullshit: *I'm okay, I'm fine.* Worse, though, was hearing the truth: she felt hopeless and alone. At a certain point, it was easier to just not answer the phone.

WHAT DOES GRIEF LOOK LIKE?

For starters, grief usually comes with some kind of tangible *primary* loss. It can be loss of mobility, energy, or appearance if dealing with health. It can be loss of a loved one, loss of a job, loss of a marriage. Even in depression, there is loss of the ability to feel just about anything. Caregivers of people who are ill lose companionship they counted on. People who experience miscarriage and infertility experience the loss of a dream of the future. These are the key primary losses a person may experience during grief:

• LOSS OF IDENTITY

We often underestimate how much we rely on easy narratives about who we are in the world until we're blindsided by a primary loss that strips us bare of them.

• LOSS OF COMPANIONSHIP

Our most difficult times often, at their core, are about a significant loss of companionship. Losing someone really close to us to death or significant illness or divorce can radically shift the make-up of our interior, intimate lives and our days. When the person we talk to the most, confide in, get opinions from, and love the deepest is gone, the hole that is left behind is vast and aching beyond measure.

• LOSS OF COMMUNITY

Loss and transition affect not only our most intimate relationships; they change our community as well, and that change usually feels really lonely. We may lose the friends and family of our loved one that is gone. We may lose people we thought we were close to because they don't know what to do or say. We can also isolate ourselves because *we* fear what our community might do or say, or because we don't have the emotional or physical energy to engage.

• LOSS OF CONFIDENCE

People who've been fired, who are dealing with a new illness, who are getting divorced, you name it—loss can create some of the most demanding responsibilities in our lives about our well-being, medical and legal options, our finances, where we'll live, or how we'll raise our children, exactly at a time when we have the fewest emotional reserves to learn and cope.

• LOSS OF ECONOMIC SECURITY

Loss can create economic stress—like increased health-care costs, the cost of divorce attorneys, loss of income, child-care costs, and a host of other expenses. One woman struggling to carry the costs of infertility treatments put it this way: "It's hard to accept a dinner invitation when what it will cost would pay for my blood draw."

Accompanying these primary losses are *secondary losses* that are more subtle, and often more difficult emotionally to deal with. However, and this is great news for our purposes, the emotional effects of these secondary losses can, with the support of friends, feel less hurtful over time. Here is a list of secondary losses, which are emotions, we experience when life gets hard:

HOPELESS: THE THING ABOUT GRIEF is THAT it CAN SEEM LIKE IT WILL NEVER, EVER END.

And in a number of ways, it doesn't. As anyone in the grief world knows, you don't get over loss. You learn to live with it. But until that happens, the light at the end of the tunnel is not a thing—or if it is, it's just barely visible on the best days.

SCARED: Fear often accompanies loss, illness, divorce, or any kind of transition, because you have no idea what's ahead of you. You end up worrying about the worst that could happen (and, thanks to the magic of the Internet, worrying is easier than ever before).

VULNERABLE: If your illness or treatment has caused you to look different, your appearance elicits concern (and questions, and strange looks), turning your rituals of everyday life, like grocery shopping, into a public spectacle. Even if you don't look different on the outside, news of a change, like divorce or job loss or fertility struggles, invites speculation that can make your life feel like fodder for gossip.

ASHAMED: Grief, fear, and our deepest feelings of failure can make us blame ourselves for causing what happened or, at least, failing to cope with it. Shame makes us feel unentitled to our own grief and fears. It looks like this:

What does experiencing loss, hopelessness, fear, vulnerability, and shame mean about receiving help?

"Asking Makes ME FEEL LiKE a BuRDEN."

When in the thick of our rough times, we can feel utterly undeserving of love and attention and think we're just taking and taking, being a burden. Even if we're comfortable asking for help in normal circumstances, many of us would rather suffer in silence than reach out for help at our worst.

"I DON'T EVEN KNOW WTF I NEED."

People who are suffering may not even know what they need until it sneaks up on them, and they realize they've been surviving for three days on Diet Coke and Twizzlers. Often, when we're suffering, outsiders see our work projects suffering, circles under our eyes getting darker, and dishes piling up in the sink more quickly than we do.

"I'M OVERWHELMED."

Crying for days on end, feeling numb, not sleeping for weeks, pretending to not be grieving so other people feel more comfortable around you—it's all exhausting. Keeping a lid on the chaos we call "life" is hard enough as it is, but then when we're at our lowest, and possibly consumed with a host of additional responsibilities related to our difficult time, life becomes one big tornado of unmanaged to-dos like laundry, shopping, cleaning, kids, and so on. Projects at work and at home don't stop just because your world did. Figuring out what needs to be done, and then, who can do it—which means assigning and coordinating jobs, managing people's feelings around jobs they're given, and dealing with the occasional lack of follow-through—is enough to make anyone want to crawl into a hole and do nothing.

THE UPSHOT?

IF a PERSON is SOBBING OVER a PILE of DISHES and a PILE of BILLS—
and WHAT FEELS LIKE a PILE of RUBBLE THAT WAS FORMERLY THEIR LIFE—
IT CAN FEEL PAINFUL and EVEN POINTLESS to ASK FOR HELP.

This means that as a caring bystander, you have the opportunity—and the responsibility—to show up and offer help without being asked. Yes, this can feel really awkward and uncomfortable when you're not used to it. But if you're worried that you've screwed up in trying to offer support, said the wrong thing, or felt like the biggest idiot—remember that you're not feeling half as terrible as the person at the center of it.

REACHING OUT and FUMBLING is OFTEN FAR BETTER THAN NOT REACHING OUT at ALL.

PART TWO:

THE THREE TOUCHSTONES OF SHOWING UP

CHAPTER 3:
your KINDNESS
IS YOUR CREDENTIAL

"Having a serious illness can feel very isolating.
The worst thing someone can do is to do and say
nothing for fear of doing or saying the wrong
thing. That just deepens those feelings of isolation."
—Terry, who had stage 3 colon cancer

Well, this is what this *feels like,* thought Maddie, as she cleared
her desk of paper clips and dumped the box of glitter pens into
her computer bag. (With all the years of service she had given,
she figured she deserved some freakin' pens.) *I've seen this
happen enough times, I should've known it would happen to me
eventually.* She spent a couple of hours writing down important

contacts and looking at examples of work she was proud of before slipping them into her bag. But she couldn't escape without first enduring the dreaded walk of shame.

Keep your head up, like it was any other day, she told herself. She walked through the corridor of glass offices on the eleventh floor, each one filled with colleagues who, under normal circumstances, would probably look up and nod, smile, give her some kind of hand signal about getting drinks later.

BUT INSTEAD,

THERE WAS MIKE, HER LUNCH PAL, LOOKING DETERMINEDLY THROUGH HIS FILE DRAWER.

THERE WAS JUANITA, TYING HER SHOELACE.

THERE WAS BELLE, FASCINATED BY THE RIVETING SCENE OUTSIDE HER WINDOW.

As she walked out, Maddie wished she'd understood what getting canned felt like sooner, because she was pretty sure she had been one of those avoiders. And she wished she had known that it wouldn't have taken much to offer a small gesture, a token of kindness—anything instead of this whole lot of nothing.

Billionaire businessman and former mayor of New York City Michael Bloomberg was asked about being fired from Solomon Brothers. He said he still remembers every person who reached out to him when he was let go. On the other hand, he said, he can't remember any of the people who called when he was promoted. That experience taught him to take an admired colleague who'd been fired out to lunch, in the most visible part of a restaurant.

Maybe because our lives can get more and more mundane the older we get, we find that what sustains us over the long haul—past all the breakups and professional screwups and weight gain and hair loss—is not the glittery connections we make when feeling on top of the world, but those we forge when we're at our lowest.

At its most basic, being supportive is all about having concern for our fellow human beings, a concern that leads to some kind of comforting action. With that,

MEET OUR FIRST TOUCHSTONE OF SHOWING UP: Your KINDNESS IS YOUR CREDENTIAL.

WHY Kindness MATTERS

The value of simple kindness can be hard to accept when you're trying to learn the Perfect Way to comfort someone, especially when you're anxious about what *not* to do or say. This is why Dr. Charles Garfield, founder of the Shanti Project, which trains volunteers to care for the sick, opens up his training with the following: "Everyone wants skills. *How to say this? How to do that?* But when people are dying, no amount of skills will earn you trust like the kindness that brings you to them in the first place. If you take nothing else from this training, take this: Your kindness is your credential."

How DO PEOPLE who CARE GET PAST that STIGMA and ACTUALLY SHOW UP?

At its core, kindness is a total absence of ego and self-interest in doing something for someone else. The defining feature of kindness is that it comes unsolicited, and in its most awe-inspiring moments, it comes to the aid of those who are shunned. People who experience loss through suicide also experience stigmatized loss, and many of them have participated in Kelsey's research.

Their examples of support show that when it comes to reaching out, smooth talk isn't a requirement. As one woman described:

> *"It wasn't easy for people to speak to me about my mother's suicide. It certainly wasn't easy for my cousin, who was clearly reading her condolences off a script she wrote. In fact, her demonstration of effort mattered more to me than whatever it is she said. Every gesture was like rain falling on drought-stricken land, because I was just deprived of the wealth of condolences that people usually receive when someone dies."*

ALL OUR DIFFICULT TIMES involve SOME DEGREE of SHAME, FEAR, and LONELINESS. AT TIMES LIKE THAT, WE DON'T NEED ANYONE to IMPRESS US OR SKILLFULLY TALK US OUT OF OUR PAIN. WE MOSTLY JUST NEED the KINDNESS that COMPELS ANYONE to TRY.

WHY KINDNESS?

Kindness comes from a basic social emotion: compassion. But what is compassion, exactly? There are a ton of competing definitions and theories about compassion (and empathy and altruism and sympathy and, yes, kindness). A definition of compassion that we like comes from researchers at the University of Michigan's Compassion Lab:

COMPASSION is to NOTICE, FEEL, and RESPOND.

First, we have to *notice*, and as simple as that sounds, we miss opportunities to show compassion all the time, because we can easily fail to notice someone's pain or fear. Seeing or anticipating someone's difficulty is a clear first step in providing them comfort.

We also have to *feel* for that person. This is what emotions expert Dr. Paul Ekman calls EMOTIONAL RESONANCE, and it is not to be confused with "identical resonance," where someone feels the exact thing as someone else. That person's support would be highly unhelpful. If you see someone's hand on fire, for example,

AAAAAAAH
HH HH,
HH HH!

AAAAAAAH
HH HH
HH HH!

Unhelpful.

and feel your hand burn just as intensely, then your capacity to fetch some ice and treat your friend is greatly diminished, because you're focusing on your own flaming hand.

INSTEAD, EMOTIONAL RESONANCE is WHEN you FEEL ENOUGH to BE CONCERNED, BUT NOT ENOUGH to REQUIRE GETTING YOUR OWN SUPPORT, TOO.

And finally, when you notice and feel for someone's pain, you *respond* with a supportive emotion or gesture. Political scientist Kristin Monroe, who explores the development of moral courage in her work, gives us valuable steps to understanding the act of compassion. To summarize, Monroe suggests a compassionate response is something we *do*, not just think about. Its benefit is solely for the other person, and the act might even diminish our welfare without any expectation of recognition on our part.

That's a pretty heroic list, which is why Monroe defines this set of qualities as "heroic compassion." To be clear, such diminishment is not about forking over our savings, our home, or quitting our jobs to help anyone in need at any personal cost. It is, however, about inconveniencing yourself for someone else.

We've all fallen short of being heroic in our compassion. Emily may "feel" for her neighbor's exhaustion after having a second baby, but she hasn't actually done anything that has positive consequences for her. Why? Because Emily is overwhelmed with work right now and hasn't made helping her neighbor a priority.

please don't judge her.

Sometimes, we just can't do the right thing. Sometimes it's because we don't care enough about the welfare of a particular person to inconvenience ourselves, and sometimes it's just because life gets in the way. The way we see it:

1. WE DON'T HAVE the CAPACITY to REACH OUT to EVERY SINGLE PERSON in NEED.

2. BUT, in REALITY, WE CAN USUALLY REACH OUT MORE than WE THINK, and IT GETS EASIER WITH PRACTICE.

Compassion gets easier because it's rewarding, and just like little rats that learn how to navigate their way out of a maze with treats, we humans are motivated by positive reinforcement too. You don't have to believe in karma to understand that physiological, neurological, and hormonal changes occur when we do something kind for someone else (they are scientifically proven). We think that by noticing these physiological and psychological (and we'll throw in moral) rewards of compassion, we're more apt to do good for others, because we are more likely to do what feels good.

Sure, your aunt Gail may have noticed you didn't send a thank-you note for her wedding gift. But if you haven't spoken to Aunt Gail in twenty years, and you find out her second husband, Harold, has died, you may wonder if you should reach out. She wouldn't necessarily notice if you didn't, but the point is: What would *you* feel if you did?

And, finally, while it's pretty obvious, it's worth stating because it's so important to our happiness: being kind in your relationships makes your relationships stronger and makes you a happier person. All that knowledge should help tilt the scale away from the cons of reaching out (fear, inconvenience) toward the pro side (happiness, better relationships).

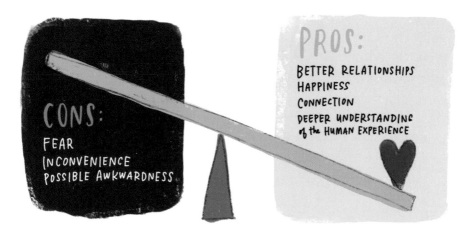

WHAT COMPASSION FEELS LIKE

So let's say you are feeling (heroically) ready to be compassionate. Fantastic. In chapters 4, 5, and 6 we explore what compassionate behavior looks like. For now, we explore the nature of compassion: the thing that compels us to inconvenience ourselves, maybe even skip that one *really* good yoga class with the really good teacher, in order to help out someone we care for.

At its core, compassion is *the acceptance of suffering*. That does not mean full detachment, in which you don't give a damn, like "hey, stuff happens, move on." And it's not an intellectual acceptance of suffering that has you looking at someone's personal tragedy through a cold haze of statistics. "Well, you know, only one out of five wind up . . ." Rather, compassion is the acceptance that awful stuff can happen to any of us. In fact, that bad things happen to good people *all the time*.

At the same time, compassion does not mean having a freakout or wincing at somebody's suffering, which feels more like pity than compassion.

ACKNOWLEDGING SOMEONE'S PAIN BY FEELING FOR THEM, BUT NOT ACTUALLY FEELING WITH THEM, is the OPPOSITE OF SUPPORTIVE COMPASSION.

People with disabilities and the elderly get this a lot too, as though they have suffered a permanent, chronic, and entirely negative change that makes them someone different. As if their whole personhood has vanished in the face of this awful, horrible thing that they're now living with.

COMPASSION ≠ PITY.

When you recognize that bad things happen to good people, and also, that bad things actually happen to *you*—it creates a connection around suffering that is a two-way relationship between equals. Compassion is not a relationship built on a notion of one always-messed-up person matched with one always-saving-the-world person. It is built upon each of us being messed up in many points of our lives.

EMPATHY WORKOUT: GETTING in the WELL

The greatest comfort comes when we're able to climb down into the "well of suffering" with a fellow human being. Here are two mental tricks to help you get down in there and feel *with* instead of *for:*

- Every time you feel for someone else's pain, imagine a time when you were feeling similarly. Don't dwell on that feeling, but touch upon it briefly and then let that personal pain go, returning to your focus on the other person.

- Remember the person you feel sad for is a whole person, made up of way more than their current situation. Conjure up their positive qualities, like their tenacity, their humor, their work drive—things that you believe will help get them through this shitty or scary time, and that continue to make them a remarkable person. And if you don't know them well, imagine they have these qualities. Because chances are, they do.

SCENARIO 1: You see a man in his seventies or eighties moving slowly up a steep hill while walking his dog. There might be a couple of things you can think:

- *Oh, that poor guy is walking with a cane, so slowly. It must be hard that it takes so long to get anywhere. I feel so sorry for him.*

  OR

- *Wow, this guy is inspiring. This is a tough hill—I hope I can be like him when I get older.*

SCENARIO 2: You're at a neighborhood party, where typically everyone is coupled up, their kids at home with a sitter. A new neighbor shows up, who's recently widowed. She heads over to the makeshift wine bar and pours herself some sauvignon blanc. You have some options on what to think:

- Pity her for being alone, without a spouse.

  OR

- Feel interested and admire her for her bravery, recalling an instance when, say, you were a chickenshit coward and didn't come to this party last year because your husband, Tim, was out of town. Feeling inspired by her gumption, you surmise that she's pretty badass, and maybe you even approach her. Not because you're doing her any special favors, but because you respect her choice, you think she's probably pretty cool, and you sympathize with how it feels to come to a party alone.

How are COMPASSION and EMPATHY DIFFERENT?

The difference between compassion and empathy may seem irrelevant when deciding on whether or not to take a casserole to your sick neighbor. But they are different concepts, and it can be useful to understand the distinction when attempting to cultivate either or both.

We'll spare you the scholarly debates about the difference between compassion and empathy and give you our conclusion.

We consider *compassion* to be the heart's natural, instinctive response to the pain of others. It's most likely to occur when you encounter a person in a difficult situation very similar to one you have suffered. You know what it felt like when your husband left you, so you naturally feel compassion for your coworker when the same thing happens to her. *Empathy* is when you use your imagination to expand your ability to feel compassion for people in situations beyond those you have experienced, maybe even in situations completely different from those you have known. It's a useful mental tool for developing more compassion.

Compassion   EMPATHY

COMPASSION = NOTICE, Feel, RESPOND
EMPATHY = COMPASSION + IMAGINATION

Here's an example that might help to make the distinction clear. Imagine that, like Kelsey, you're a breast cancer survivor. Survivors often hear, both directly and indirectly, that they shouldn't worry about recurrence or be afraid of their disease, because with the current treatments available, "breast cancer isn't as serious as it used to be." As a survivor, you dread hearing this, because it diminishes your very real, very scary experience. To you, these fears are more than valid.

Now imagine that you, the breast cancer survivor, are talking with your friend who's getting divorced. This friend is afraid that at age fifty, she'll never find love again. But your fifty-year-old cousin is fighting men off with a stick. Celebrity magazines are full of women who are dating younger men. And remember Samantha on *Sex and the City*? Guys everywhere. Plus, your friend is a great catch. So you feel pretty strongly that her fears are unwarranted and maybe even a little irrational. In fact, you're kind of annoyed at having to tend to her feelings of worry, and instead of comforting her, you just want to tell her to stop freaking out about it, because she's going to be fine.

In this example, it's easy for you to feel compassion for your fellow breast cancer survivors' fears of recurrence, but you don't have a lot of compassion for your divorcing friend's fears that she'll be alone forever. It's one thing to feel for someone who is

in a similar situation to us—that's compassion. But feeling for someone in a different situation requires empathy. Empathy is the ability to extract the core experience of a situation we know, which, in this case, is about fear of the worst-case scenario, and then to use that information to imagine and feel what it might be like to be in a situation that appears entirely different. And the more we practice empathy, the easier it is to access feelings of compassion for people in situations that appear far different from our own.

EMPATHY WORKOUT: FROM COMPASSION TO EMPATHY

Here, you can practice using your experience with one kind of situation to imagine how it might feel to go through a seemingly entirely different experience.

Think about three really tough situations you have been through. Could be miscarriage, loss, illness, a breakup, you name it.

Now, think about three other situations that you maybe have not personally experienced. Could be infertility, divorce, loss of a job, or something very specific going on for someone you know right now.

What might the situation you've directly experienced have in common with the one that you haven't? Pair them up, and consider these prompts to help you get specific:

- Loss of community

- Fear and emotional overwhelm

- Loss of identity

- Shame

- Financial difficulty

The more we employ our empathic imagination, the more we are able to notice and *appreciate* other people's suffering. We don't need to walk a mile in another person's shoes to realize when another human being needs support. We simply use our power to notice, feel, respond, and imagine what someone might be going through.

 IF YOU CARE, YOUR CARE BELONGS.

Most of us recognize that caring is important, yet we still question: Does the suffering person even care that *I* care? And even more vexing: Would the suffering, grieving, freaked-out person feel like my support is butting in? Chances are, you have wrestled with questions like the following:

- A neighbor's spouse died. You don't know his name, but you greet and chitchat with him. Should you say anything?

- An old friend from twenty years ago has been diagnosed with cancer. Do you reach out?

- A colleague you admire just got fired. What can you do to show your support without embarrassing him?

- Your good friend had a miscarriage. How do you know if she wants to talk about it?

There is no algorithm that can exactly specify who is "qualified" to reach out and when. However, it's safe to say that no matter what your relationship is to someone in a difficult time, the "appropriateness" of your overture is in great part determined by the values you bring to it.

Think about the things that have made you cringe when others have approached you in a time of suffering. The bad moments almost always boil down to you having to deal with people's reactions to your situation.

IN ADDITION to YOUR OWN PAIN,
you FIND YOURSELF CONTEMPLATING QUESTIONS LIKE:

WHAT IF SHE WANTS TO USE MY CRUMBLING SHITSHOW OF A MARRIAGE AS GOSSIP TO FEEL BETTER ABOUT HER MARRIAGE?

WHAT IF THEY THINK I'M SELFISH FOR WANTING TO PURSUE IVF?

WHAT IF HE GETS ALL JUDGEY ABOUT THE CANCER TREATMENT I DECIDED ON?

ONE THING MANY OF US LEARN,
WITH a LOT OF TEARS and REGRET, IS THAT:

WE CAN'T TRUST OUR PAIN and FEARS WITH EVERYONE.

A lot of us can be judgmental. And a lot of times that's okay. Our opinions are a source of personality. Compassion should not make you vapid. But when it comes to the people around us who are vulnerable, being too judgey about people's pain will make people feel less secure in sharing their personal problems.

AND THAT'S BECAUSE... PEOPLE DON'T WANT TO BE BLAMED FOR THEIR PROBLEMS, and THEY DON'T WANT TO HAVE TO DEFEND THEIR CHOICES.

To help you feel like you are a *trustworthy* person with someone's vulnerability, consider the following:

- Each time I judge or gossip about someone's pain, anyone who witnesses that will be less likely to entrust me with their pain.

- Each time I connect with others by judging someone else's pain, I collude with people who likely can't hang with *my* pain.

To help you overcome that judgmental attitude that can creep up on all of us—especially when exasperated, wanting to fill up airtime, or just being plain thoughtless (it happens)—we recommend these three mantras:

- I will look at people's personal difficulty with compassion and empathy.

- I will not judge people for their personal difficulty.

- I will not gossip about people's personal difficulty.

COMPASSION'S F-WORDS: FOIST and FRET

The best of values that we bring to helping doesn't prevent some of us from being a tad bit annoying in how we help. To anyone who has seen the "always look for the helpers" quote from Mr. Rogers online, this observation may sound like blasphemy.

But there's a big difference between people who are kind and helpful (which is who Fred Rogers is talking about) and "chronic helpers." Chronic helpers might be looking to use someone else's needy situation to improve their self-worth. If our desire to help is motivated by insecurity, as described on page 37, then being the "perfect helper" might be a tempting accolade to pursue. Two tendencies most exhibit the "needy" helper that lies within many of us:

FOISTER:

Someone who pushes themselves onto someone in their difficult time with a lot of advice and unappreciated overtures.

FRETTER:

Someone who anxiously reacts with neediness around someone in their difficult time.

YOU DON'T WANT a PERSON in PAIN TO FEEL OBLIGATED BY YOUR OVERTURES, JUST SUPPORTED BY THEM.

Both the Fretter and Foister place a lot of emphasis on their own helping abilities. But while Foisters are narcissistic—that is, unable to see the needs of the suffering person—and are largely concerned with their own opinions and agendas, Fretters are acutely attuned to the facial expressions and emotions of people who are in pain. They just feel incapable of helping them through it without a lot of assurance that they're doing a great job.

You might recognize yourself as a Fretter if you find yourself asking a lot of very specific questions of the person in need about how to help, and asking for assurance on how you are already helpful. Don't be surprised if you, a reader of this very kind of book, find yourself identifying with this tendency—both of us do, too.

You might recognize yourself as a Foister if you tend to feel that others are ungrateful for your help. You might feel offended by people not taking your well-meaning advice or following up on resources that you provided, or feel unappreciated when people in crisis are not texting or phoning you back. You might notice that people shut down, stop sharing feelings with you, and possibly avoid you.

Many of us are Fretters or Foisters—it's good to want to give effective care to our loved ones. So don't feel bad if you recognize either of these tendencies in your help. But if you want to do things a little differently—and likely more effectively—here are some options:

	INSTEAD OF THIS	**TRY THIS**
FOISTER	"Why didn't you tell me?"	"I am so sorry. How are you?"
	"I really think you'd feel better if you came to the annual family picnic. Don't let all those babies get to you. Maybe it will even boost your fertility levels."	"Since being around kids is so hard right now, but it's really important that you be a part of this, would you want to help me decorate the place beforehand?"
	"Don't be such a downer. You should come out with us. It will be fun. This will be good for you."	"If you're not up for socializing, can I come by with a trashy movie and we can just not talk much?"
FRETTER	"I called you yesterday and didn't hear back from you. I just need you to phone me and let me know that everything is all right."	"I'm just leaving you a message (text, email) to say hello. No need to call me back."
	"I didn't hear back from you. Did you get my package?"	Try not mentioning the package and just presume it arrived.
	"I wanted to get you a pair of slippers for the hospital, but I didn't know what color you'd like, or if wool was okay. Is it okay that I didn't get you anything? Or can I get you something else?"	Buy the slippers and hope the thought itself is appreciated. You don't care if they wind up in the hands of someone else at Goodwill.
	"I was hoping to get you a gift certificate from a local restaurant. What's the nearest one to you? Do they deliver? How much should it be for?"	Look up the important information, don't sweat the details, and just send the certificate. (But be clear on any diet restrictions first.)

TRUST:
SOMETIMES, WE DON'T CARE.
NOT ENOUGH, ANYWAY.

It's true. As we mentioned earlier in the example of Emily and her neighbor, the new parent, sometimes we're not affected by someone's hardship enough to inconvenience ourselves for them. We couldn't go on with the daily routines of our lives if we reached out to every person with a hint of suffering in our day. That's normal.

Sometimes we care, but for the wrong reasons, like when there's a tiny bit of satisfaction in witnessing someone else's downfall, or when we just want details for the sake of knowing them. Such situations are not nice, but none of us is nice all the time. It's just important that we know when we're not feeling like doing the right thing, and in those cases it's best to stay away from the situation.

If, on the other hand, you've always felt for your neighbor Suzie, for example, who never sweated through her yoga pants, always kept her kids in matching outfits, and managed a high-powered career—yet often seemed a bit unhappy and pressed to be perfect—you may find yourself deeply caring when her life unravels in divorce. Maybe because you've been there yourself, when you lost your job and learned that nothing in life is like it's supposed to be, and what it feels like to publicly "fail." Well, then, maybe you can reach out. Even if you're "just" a neighbor, you're actually more than that. You're someone who genuinely cares, so trust that.

TRUST in COMPASSION FOR YOURSELF.

We all benefit from feeling more compassion for others. There are exceptions, however. And that's why in Kelsey's Empathy Bootcamps, there is considerable discussion on how much help we can actually give.

Three instances should give us pause before diving in to help someone else:

1. SOMETIMES LIFE GETS in the WAY, and CRISES OFTEN HAPPEN at the MOST INCONVENIENT TIMES.

   Your work colleague finds out she has cancer right before a major product launch. Your best friend's relationship is crumbling when you have a major deadline. Just when it feels extra challenging to take care of ourselves, we're sometimes called upon to take care of others. And when we're stressed, research shows we are less likely to feel empathy for other people.

2. THE PERSON YOU CARE ABOUT is ACTUALLY REALLY HARD to CARE FOR.

   Their issues, like with major mental illness, addiction, and dementia, for example, are way more emotionally and financially demanding than you, a normal human being, can handle.

3. THERE ARE PEOPLE *in* OUR LIVES WHO ARE TAKERS, WHO WILL ALWAYS WANT MORE THAN WE CAN REASONABLY GIVE.

They are, as personal development author Mark Manson calls them, "emotional vampires," people who have no filter on their emotions for even the smallest of life's grievances. They are always wronged, always disappointed in others, and they are really hard people to give to.

In these moments, show compassion for yourself. Recognize that maybe you (a) *can't* do it all, or (b) don't *want* to do it all. Not because you hate being inconvenienced (since helping others will always be at least a *tad* inconvenient), but because you recognize you can't give without feeling depleted and, thus, resentful. Use the following cues to help guide your caring actions for others, and your caring actions for yourself.

- NOTICE WHAT'S GOING ON INSIDE OF YOU.

  Your irritation might not be the result of any real demands of the suffering person. They may have asked for nothing at all. It might simply be about the current level of stress you feel in your own life.

- TAKE A MOMENT *to* NOTICE YOUR STRESS.

  Is it impacting your empathy? A few deep breaths can de-escalate your stress-induced irritation at someone else's suffering.

- **TAKE A MOMENT for SELF-INVENTORY.**

  What do I feel prepared to do for this person? Recognize that this notion can change over time. What do I feel obligated to do for this person versus what I *want* to do for this person? And practice this mind-set: *I am not obliged to do this. I want to do this.*

- **TAKE A LOOK at CHAPTER 5.**

  We describe ways to limit the pressure of what you feel you *should* do and give you ways to think about what you can do—easily, and without undue stress.

If you want to be there for others to honor or maybe even deepen your relationships, consider how to offer a level of support that will help you do those things. However, you should also feel entitled to set limits on caring for people. It's perfectly reasonable to recognize that you can't give everything that *you think* you should give. What's more, you can't always give what *others* think you should give.

KELSEY Says: *There are people in our lives with really big, chronic problems. Addiction, severe mental illness, dementia, you name it. When there is deep love for people who are in deep pain, our natural instinct is to want to fix it, no matter at what personal cost. For years I struggled with the*

competing feelings of guilt, love, and anger that had me questioning every day what I could do to help my mother who had severe mental illness. Our book can't adequately help you deal with this level of crisis. We can only acknowledge the real difficulty of your situation. To help you figure out a way forward, try seeking out help from professionals. A lifesaver for me, a self-proclaimed nonjoiner, was joining a support group for people who shared my situation. I found understanding and much needed forgiveness for fumbling in a less-than-perfect (oftentimes horrible) situation.

THE BOTTOM LINE: BEING YOURSELF is PERFECT ENOUGH.

Compassion for others isn't fully possible if we don't also have compassion for ourselves. *Nobody is perfect*—not you, not the people you lean on to get your own support. Being kind does not mean you are not allowed to also be a Fretter or a Foister. You may have big problems setting boundaries, or you may have a really full, stressful life right now, which makes it really hard to change or add something to your routine. What we really hope is for you to simply feel more aware of the human tendencies that can get in the way of fully expressing compassion: stress in the face of inconvenience, fear of setting boundaries, and pressure to do things "perfectly."

IF WE ARE to FULLY GIVE, WE MUST DO SO BY **FIRST** GIVING COMPASSION to OURSELVES.
BECAUSE WHAT SOMEONE *in* CRISIS REALLY NEEDS IS NOT YOUR SKILLED PERFECTION, BUT YOU.

CHAPTER 4:
LISTENING
SPEAKS VOLUMES

"My dad asked questions like, 'Can you hang in there? Can you go to counseling?' He was trying to explore things I could do for the marriage to work it out, as opposed to just being receptive and listening: 'How are you doing? How are you feeling?'"

—Tina, who went through a divorce

Victoria was married to a cheater. It wasn't her fault, but there it was, plain and simple. Her husband: the cad. How long had she known? Well, she'd been married to Doug seven years; six years earlier he'd passed out on the couch with his laptop open and a beer in his hand. She'd gone over, fondly, to cover him up, and there it was, for everyone to see: *Tuesday at lunch? Airport Sheraton? Miss you, big boy. Suzanne.*

Victoria had closed the browser and put the computer away. She'd never mentioned it. But when she would periodically check his email over the years, there were other women too. Carissa. Heather. Molly.

WAS SHE PATHETIC?
HER SISTER CERTAINLY THOUGHT SO.

YOUR HUSBAND IS TERRIBLE. HE CHEATS. AND WHAT'S THIS $11,000 CREDIT CARD BILL? WHAT THE HELL IS HE BUYING FOR $11,000? HE'S NOT SPENDING IT ON YOU — YOUR SHIRT IS FROM TARGET!

WHAT SHOULD I DO?

GET A DIVORCE.

At year eight, Victoria thought maybe having children would help. But they were now $60,000 in debt, and something needed to shock this guy into finding a steady job. She decided to bring it up over pot roast, Doug's favorite. Doug came in, kissed her, and had two servings.

"I think we should have a baby," Victoria said, heart pounding.

Doug blinked.

"BUT HONEY, I'M LEAVING YOU FOR DOROTHY," DOUG SAID. SO THERE YOU GO, VICTORIA HAD HER ANSWER: DIVORCE.

After months of legal hassles, gradually setting out on her own, and feeling like a wreck every day, an unexpected old friend reemerged: Anna. Victoria had sort of forgotten about Anna. They had known each other in college and stayed in touch off and on. Anna had been a brash, out-there sort of person who always dragged people to dance class. But when Anna heard Victoria was going through a divorce, she came over with lasagna and a magnum of Yellowtail and stayed the night.

"What you don't need," Anna said, "is an empty house."

Anna was twice divorced—a connoisseur. Victoria had to admit Anna was right. The emptiness of her house mocked her constantly. The quiet was another form of sadness, ever blooming.

So Anna kept coming over, and Victoria kept letting her. Anna brought burritos, macaroni, baked ziti, and potatoes au gratin. They would hang out in the kitchen and have tea. Anna didn't tell Victoria that Doug was an ass or that she had wasted her youth.

"You married him, after all," Anna said. "There must have been *something* good."

Victoria nodded. There *were* good things. Which is why she so often found herself sobbing to her new—no, old—friend.

Victoria knew she was better without him, but it didn't feel that way. Anna said it wouldn't, not for a long, long time. But then it would, she said. After a long while, Victoria made the choice to believe her.

Knowing how bad it can feel to hear the wrong thing, and how easy it can be to say the wrong thing, many of us would rather remain silent and walk away from an emotionally difficult situation. Even if we know from experience how comforting it can be to have someone to talk to, when we're in the position to provide such comfort, that conversation can easily feel too overwhelming to handle. Thankfully, these conversations get much easier with practice, and they can pretty much guarantee us the absolute best way to build deep, trusting, unshakable relationships—the kind most of us can use more of.

MEET OUR SECOND TOUCHSTONE of SHOWING UP: LISTENING SPEAKS VOLUMES.

The best way to have a conversation with someone in a difficult time is not in the talking, but in the listening.

AND THANKFULLY, it's MUCH EASIER to **LISTEN** THAN IT IS TO FIND THAT ELUSIVE "**USEFUL**" THING TO SAY.

As the mom of a child with cystic fibrosis told us:

> *"People think that by listening, they aren't contributing to the conversation. Totally wrong. Listening to me talk about this horrible disease is one of the biggest gifts that I can receive."*

The enormous value of listening is probably not news to most of us, but when the shit hits the fan and your friend is in pain, "How can I make this better?" is a totally natural reaction.

IT'S INSTINCTIVE to WANT to SAY SOMETHING—ANYTHING—in THE HOPES THAT YOU MIGHT IMPROVE THE SITUATION.
YOU'LL COME OUT OF THIS EVEN STRONGER.
I MEAN, AT LEAST IT'S NOT CANCER!
THIS IS JUST LIKE THE TIME I GOT FOOD POISONING ON THAT CRUISE.
WHAT DO THE LAB RESULTS SAY?
HOW ARE YOU GOING TO HANDLE THE KIDS?
YOU SHOULD TRY A RAW FOOD DIET.
...OR ACUPUNCTURE. PROBABLY BOTH.

Yet, before diving into rescue mode with advice, alternative ways of looking at things, or asking a lot of clarifying questions—all the things you want to be *really cautious* about doing—communication experts advise getting to a place of what they call "emotional resonance" (see our discussion of emotional resonance on page 60). That means using the act of listening to tune in to how someone is feeling about her situation.

Ask people what matters most about listening and they will inevitably tell you it's having someone hear your experience without judgment. What's more, listening actually helps a person better understand their experience in the course of telling it. One man from an Empathy Bootcamp put it this way:

> *"As the relationship with my wife started to go south, my family and friends listened to me patiently over many years. I had to talk it through several times (ad nauseam) in order to come to the best decision about what to do."*

LEARNING TO SHUT UP

The first thing to get really good at when wanting to listen is also probably the biggest hurdle to listening, which is sitting "dumbly" quiet while someone else talks.

WHILE YOU'RE LISTENING, YOU'RE FOCUSED ENTIRELY ON WHAT THE PERSON IS SAYING, and YOU'RE NOT SIMULTANEOUSLY THINKING ABOUT HOW YOU'RE GOING TO RESPOND. (YES. THIS IS a CRAZY NOTION FOR MANY OF US.) IN MOST CASES, THIS IS THE BEST KIND OF LISTENING WE CAN DO.

So after your friend shares a piece of bad or scary news, practice waiting three seconds before responding. This sounds like a short amount of time, but in reality, it can feel like an eternity if you're not used to it. So prepare to exercise restraint, and prepare for uncomfortable silence.

When THE SILENCE OF LISTENING is UNCOMFORTABLE, IT'S NOT BECAUSE SILENCE is a PROBLEM. IT'S BECAUSE YOU AREN'T USED to IT.

A couple of things may happen: either the silence continues—and you both learn that sitting together in the introspective quiet, feeling how *life can be hard*, is actually pretty profound and amazing (rather than shallow and awkward)—or your friend may very well fill up the silence by talking even more about what is going on. Either thing encourages authentic communication.

To help you learn to listen better, we'll first do an inventory of some normal, common go-to responses that many of us lean on.

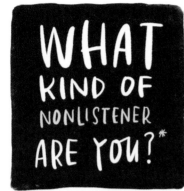

* EMILY HAS A TENDENCY TOWARD SAGE/EPIDEMIOLOGIST.
KELSEY LEANS TOWARD DOOMSAYER.

Next time you are listening to someone—about pretty much anything—take note of how you tend to respond, especially if what's being shared is a vulnerable topic. And take heart: we all have at least one of the nonlistener tendencies (and we discuss them in greater detail in this chapter and the next). Then, just practice *not* doing that thing you normally do.

You know what comes next: just stay quiet (for three whole seconds!) and listen.

EMPATHY WORKOUT: LISTEN to a FRIEND

Find a friend and practice this skill: Spend two minutes each, sharing a story of something difficult that has happened in your life. You might want to start by picking something not emotionally charged right now, but something that was a big deal in the past. Here are the rules:

THE LISTENER:

Absolutely no talking of *any* kind, even if it's just clarifying questions. You can nod and show in your face that you hear, but remember: bear the awkward silence.

THE TALKER:

Share your story and proceed on with it, even if the silence is a little unnerving.

After each of you has shared your story, consider these questions:

FOR THE TALKER:

- How did it feel to have the "space" to tell your story without interruption?

- Did the listener do something that helped you relax? How about something that made you uncomfortable?

- What is especially powerful about being listened to (especially when it's not an artificial exercise)?

FOR THE LISTENER:

- Were there times you wanted to jump in and say something while the other person was talking? What did you feel compelled to say? (This is also a really good way to identify your go-to "nonlistening" responses.)

- What was it like to stay silent throughout the story? What concerns about staying quiet did you have?

- What benefit did you get out of listening?

EMPATHY TIP: Don't worry: if you don't have an Official Listening Partner to do this exercise with, you still have a lot of opportunities to practice listening. When you actually decide to cultivate a practice of listening, you will find listening opportunities all around you. There might be a work colleague describing her return from maternity leave or a friend who is complaining about a disagreement with his neighbor—either would be a perfect opportunity to practice listening. Even in these seemingly light circumstances, you can ask some variant of "How is that for you?" and stay quiet for three seconds to see what comes up.

TYPES OF LISTENING:

The kind of listening we just described—being quiet and letting the other person talk until they have finished talking— is a lot of what really good listening is about and is called **EMPATHIC LISTENING.** Research shows that empathic listening is the most valuable kind. It establishes connection and trust and encourages people to really open up. It helps us tune in emotionally to how someone is feeling, and it involves 95 percent silence on our part. We may ask a few prompts that encourage more sharing (which we describe in more detail on page 109). It may also include nodding your head when something resonates. Mostly, however, it means encouraging someone to talk, and when she stops, allowing for three whole seconds of silence before *you* talk. This allows time for anything else she wants to say to come up, which often happens after a brief period of silence. If you jump in too soon, you may prevent her from expressing everything she wants to say.

IN ACTION, THE GOAL OF EMPATHIC LISTENING IS TO AFFECT PEOPLE *in* THIS WAY:

> "In my grief, even good advice couldn't help. Only listening did. My college roommate had lost her father years before. With her, I never felt pressure to be in a different place. She often said nothing. She just let me be in the sadness— feel it, breathe it. I had to fully let it in to let it go."
>
> —Dara, who lost her mother

There are two secondary kinds of listening that we may need to engage in when supporting someone:

FACT-FINDING LISTENING: IN FACT-FINDING LISTENING, WE WANT to REMEMBER WHAT'S BEING SAID BECAUSE THE INFORMATION *is* USEFUL.

In a casual situation, a friend may be sharing a recipe, or the name of a really good movie. We listen to remember facts that we'll need to call on in the future. In the context of hard times, this might mean getting to know the specifics of a situation to help this person later on, whether that's through relaying information to others, finding them a resource, or just because we plan on being supportive in future conversations and want to get a good handle on the situation.

But, when fact-finding, there should be a lot of room for *caution.* In Kelsey's Empathy Bootcamps, when people engage in a listening exercise and are quiet for *two whole* minutes while someone else shares their story, two things inevitably happen: (1) some people can't resist asking clarifying questions, and (2) the feedback from the talkers is that this clarifying behavior is annoying.

Of course, we feel well intentioned when asking questions, because we want our response to be grounded in a solid understanding of the situation. But this kind of listening can get in the way of sharing, because: (1) people often are looking to unload more than they are looking for a particular response, (2) fact-finding questions can divert the conversation away from what a person really wants to talk about to what the asking person wants to know, and (3) fact-finding conversations create a detached, clinical portrayal of the problem rather than an emotional one.

WHAT KIND OF LADDER DID HE FALL FROM? FOURTH RUNG, OR THIRD?

Fact-Finding LISTENING

Getting the facts can be important to your helping in the long term, but you don't usually need a lot of specific facts to comfort someone. When you do ask clarifying questions or seek information for future reference, be sure you've established some kind of trust with empathic listening first.

CRITICAL LISTENING: IN CRITICAL LISTENING, OUR MAIN GOAL Is TO ANALYZE and EVALUATE WHAT WE HEAR.

Critical listening helps us form an opinion and make a judgment and might even include a healthy amount of debate. It's something we do a lot of at work, and sometimes at brunch, but it's only occasionally helpful in the context of someone experiencing a difficult time. Critical listening in this type of scenario might involve the listener describing his own perception of the situation the person is struggling with: "It seems to me like . . ." Or it might involve the listener coming up with some explanation for why something is happening and, overall, provide a perspective that the suffering person may not have.

SINCE THE CANCER IS IN YOUR THROAT, COULD IT MEAN THAT YOU'RE NOT SPEAKING YOUR TRUTH?

Critical LISTENING

Use this listening skill with even more restraint than you would fact-finding. People can very easily experience your different perspective on a situation as a negative judgment about the perspective they already hold. That's a perfectly normal dialogue over bottomless mimosas or in a meeting, but when someone is hurting and is extra sensitive, this kind of perceived judgment can be off-putting and hurtful. Only do this when invited, and even then, use extreme caution.

EMPATHY TIP: If you are a trusted person in someone's life, you can learn what kind of listening to best use by asking this one question: "Do you want comfort or truth?" If they just want comfort, use your empathic listening skills. If they want truth, help them with some honest evaluating. Be sure to employ some empathic listening first, to tune in to what they are feeling emotionally. That will help bolster feelings of trust when it comes to any evaluative insights you might have to offer.

CONVERSATIONAL OPENERS:
WAYS to EMOTIONALLY CONNECT and LEARN MORE

Now that you've got a grasp of listening, let's bring in the second, smaller, yet harder part of a conversation: talking. Knowing what to say, and when to say it, starts with these two very simple principles of supportive communication:

1. YOU CAN'T SOLVE the PROBLEM.

2. YOU'LL NEVER KNOW HOW THEY FEEL.

YOU CAN'T SOLVE the PROBLEM
(and YOU DON'T NEED TO)

The kind of mistakes we tend to make while trying to help people can be traced to a lesson we all learned very early in life:

LOSS IS INTOLERABLE.

When someone close to us suffers a loss—whether it's of a person, a former "normal life" of being healthy, married, or employed, or an acknowledgment of what will never come, like a biological baby—often, our first instinct is to help solve the problem. We say things like "Just give it time" or "You'll have a new _____ (baby, job, partner . . .) in no time!" or "Have you tried . . . ?"

YOU'RE STILL YOUNG, YOU SHOULD TRY ONLINE DATING!

This approach works very well if someone loses their iPhone. It really *doesn't* work if someone suffers a major loss. In many cases, a grieving person will never "go back to normal" because their entire life has changed, and there's no "normal" to go back to. In these intensely difficult situations, ones that have no solution, many of our default responses to be helpful just aren't appropriate.

We have all had that sensation of looking at someone sharing a personal difficulty, and in response to our efforts to "fix" the problem with solutions or alternative ways of looking at things, we begin to see their eyes gaze down, and their arms fold across their chest. We see they are shutting down, and we feel tongue-tied, fumbling to say something—anything to make our embarrassment stop! Which often leads to us pontificating even more. In turn, our friend feels like they've just had their suffering micromanaged. And as anyone who's ever been micromanaged knows—it's *really not fun.*

YOU'LL NEVER KNOW HOW THEY FEEL.

If you've participated in life, you've suffered to some degree. Yet, despite our shared experiences, everyone goes through loss differently.

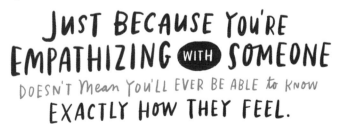

"I know how you feel" is a common saying we use to make someone feel better. Unless we're taught otherwise, it's one of those default "this is what you're supposed to say" phrases that we grow up believing is true and useful.

However, the point of empathy is not to mirror the exact experience of someone else. Empathy gives you insight into the experience of true suffering and fear, and an inkling of what that might feel like. But saying "I know how you feel" can sound dismissive of that suffering person's own, unique experience. Not one experience is like another—an illness immediately following the initial diagnosis is a very different experience from that same illness ten years out.

DIVORCE, FOR SOME PEOPLE, IS ABSOLUTELY DEVASTATING.

FOR OTHERS, IT'S A RELIEF and a REASON TO THROW A PARTY.

Any one event, at any particular point in time, for each individual, can include a whole range of emotions, including but not limited to:

What is the person you care about actually feeling? Even if you've been through something similar, you don't really know until you ask. But we know asking can be hard. Here are some places to start.

TRY ASKING "HOW ARE YOU?"

This sounds so basic, but in practice, many of us struggle with asking someone how they are doing. Depending on your relationship, you may feel unsure about how close you need to be with a person to ask how they're doing. Human nature is fickle, and you'll have to rely on your gut instinct, which, if you're scared of conversations like these, will likely tell you not to pry. As you get more practiced at this, your judgment about whether to ask will improve and you'll feel comfortable asking more often. Just remember:

NO ONE DIES FROM BEING ASKED "HOW ARE YOU?"

It can be scary to ask, but it's also true that no one has been critically injured by the question "How are you?" Most people— even those who don't care to respond with an honest answer— will appreciate it. "How are you?" is literally the most basic of follow-up questions, because it (1) acknowledges that you remember and care about what's going on, yet (2) doesn't require a long commitment to a conversation if a grieving person doesn't want to give it.

Take note of what one woman told us about her colleague's response to the loss of her mother:

"After I returned to work, no one ever spoke of what had happened. That was fine from people I didn't work closely with, but even though I understood it was probably just awkward, it was still hurtful from people I had considered friends."

WHEN TO AVOID "HOW ARE YOU?"

"How are you?" is a great way to open up a conversation, but there are times when it's a pretty safe bet that asking how somebody is will drive them crazy. This is especially true when the person you are asking is clearly distraught, or in the first few days or weeks of a significant tragedy and still in crisis. Asking the question in these times might seem to suggest that a person could be feeling any other way than horrible, and that's not very comforting to someone in distress.

IF SOMEONE'S WIFE JUST DIED, OR THEY WERE JUST DIAGNOSED WITH A BRAIN TUMOR, and YOU ASK THEM "HOW ARE YOU DOING?," THEY MAY WELL REPLY WITH SOME VERSION OF "HOW THE FUCK DO YOU THINK I'M DOING?"
WHICH, in ALL HONESTY, IS a FAIR RESPONSE.

One man told Kelsey the story of his sister-in-law, who lost her baby to sudden infant death syndrome (SIDS). In the days after the tragedy, with the entire family at home with her, his sister-in-law put a sign on her door about things to do and not do. What was the first item on the list? "Don't ask us 'How we are.'" Sometimes, especially in the initial days of a major trauma, the answer to that question is just too painfully obvious.

HOW **HARD** to PRESS?

When someone is in pain, we can ask ourselves, *How hard should I press for an honest answer?* The good news is you don't need a psych degree to get people to open up. Everyone deals with trauma in their own way, and some people just don't like to talk about their feelings. Moreover, who knows what else might be happening in someone's life? Your friend might be sick of answering questions or just not feeling well or simply exhausted. An answer of "fine" is probably not about you, so don't take it personally.

But here's another strong reason someone might not open up: they might not believe you want the real story. A woman who had a miscarriage told Kelsey: "My close family didn't bring up the loss unless I did. It would have helped me to talk about it openly if they had asked more questions and checked in more directly to see how I was feeling."

Once you feel good about the intention of asking "How are you?," here are a couple of things you can say that convey your true interest in hearing a person open up (but without being pushy):

1. "WHAT'S THAT LIKE FOR YOU?" OR "HOW'S THAT GOING FOR YOU?"

Practice this regularly. "What's that like for you?" is a great question in lieu of "How are you?" because it gives people even wider latitude for responding. That's because it could be that the person in need is obsessing over their health insurance, or attorney fees, or even about finding a moment of peace, rather than their deepest feelings.

2. "HOW ARE YOU TODAY?"

Sheryl Sandberg, COO of Facebook and author of *Lean In*, shared in a Facebook post examples of human connection during her immediate time of grief after the sudden loss of her husband. She wrote, "Even a simple 'How are you?'—almost always asked with the best of intentions—is better replaced with 'How are you, today?' . . . [because] the person knows that the best I can do right now is to get through each day."

Adding the word *today* to your question acknowledges that:

- Overall, you understand the person's life is difficult, and you're not expecting to hear a pat answer that everything is fine. That there are good days and bad days (okay, good hours and bad hours).

- It turns an overwhelming question—"How am I doing with my cancer diagnosis and life overall?"—into a totally manageable one—"How am I feeling *today*?"

How Do I Bring It Up Later, Without Making It Weird?

When encountering someone several months or more after their difficulty, a variant of asking about "today" is asking "How are you feeling *now*?" Asking about "now" allows someone to express feelings and even perspectives about their loss that can be quite different from those experienced at the initial time of loss.

Let's imagine you run into Hope—a friend you haven't seen for two years—at the mall and ask her generally:

How are you?

You

Fine, thanks. I don't know if you heard that I finished treatment for breast cancer a year ago.

HOPE

You have three options for a response:

1. "I am so sorry" (making Hope feel pitied for a condition that may not bother her as much as it once did).

2. Pretend like you didn't hear her and say, "And what else is new?"

3. Ask: "How are you doing with your diagnosis, *now*?"

You may think that asking someone how they are doing about their situation will add an extra hour to the conversation, time that maybe you don't have. But what you will find instead is that it probably just adds on an extra fifteen to twenty seconds. And we think that time is well worth what you get back in a moment of real dialogue. Besides, if the person mentioned it in the first place, they won't mind you asking, and probably even want to talk about it.

WHEN IT'S BEEN a WHILE WITH ALMOST ANY KIND OF TRANSITION, FEEL FREE to ASK, "HOW ARE YOU DOING WITH IT, NOW?"

IT'S ABOUT CURIOSITY

Asking "How are you?" is less about the three words you're asking and much more about showing a genuine interest in how someone else is feeling and what they are thinking. And many times, that may mean that what's required is not the exact words *How are you?* but something more specific that still gets you at the heart of what the person you are supporting thinks and feels (and not you.) See what we mean with this example:

I am struggling with telling John that I want a divorce.

JENNIE

Oh, I know just how you feel. When I told my ex-husband about wanting a divorce, I was afraid he'd leave me bankrupt.

LISA

Let's break this down: In fact, Jennie is struggling to tell John because he has been depressed for several years, and she doesn't want this divorce to push him over the edge. Now, Jennie doesn't know whether to tell Lisa this, or whether to let Lisa's (false) impression of the situation persist.

Let's try this again:

I am struggling with telling John that I want a divorce.

JENNIE

What's the struggle about? [Here, Lisa is convinced that finances are the source of the problem, but she resists sharing her theory and instead asks Jennie what the struggle is about. This is a very specific form of "How are you?" that involves asking a follow-up question to information that was already provided.]

Well, to be honest, he's been in a bad place emotionally for a long time, and I'm afraid this news might push him over the edge.

This time around, Lisa may be surprised by Jennie's answer, but she gets to hear and connect over Jennie's true story.

Practice listening for clues into what someone is already telling you about how they feel, and simply follow that up with "What's the [insert a version of the word the talker used] about?"

WAYS to MAKE the CONVERSATION SUPPORTIVE
JUST SAY I'M SORRY.

When we do feel compassion for someone's difficulty, and it seems to be a fair bet that that person is feeling like the situation they are in is pretty crappy, then a BIG start in the direction of reaching out with supportive kindness, and sometimes all we ever need to do, is to say the words: I'M SORRY.

When we are in the position of knowing someone's sorrow, then trust that "I'm sorry" covers a lot more ground than you'd think. With just two words, you can elegantly suggest both concern and sympathy. If this "sorry" is delivered with compassion and not with pity, then it's a validation of pain with no other agenda. And often, that acknowledgment of pain is all a suffering person needs.

Saying "I'm sorry" is so easy you probably don't believe you can get away with it.

How Could it BE OKAY to RESPOND to SOMETHING AS HEAVY AS a DEATH WITH TWO WORDS?

Trust us: you actually can. Even if all you do is communicate "I'm sorry" in a card, or even on social media, with no follow-up questions or commentary, you are doing more than fine.

Sometimes, you might wonder if you have enough of a

relationship to even say "I'm sorry." The answer is yes, yes, yes. Always. Colleagues: yes. Neighbors: yes. Even that guy next to you on the plane who's telling you he's flying to a funeral. I'm sorry! Just say it. You're acknowledging another human being's pain. You don't need an engraved invitation to entitle you to do that.

THEN THERE are TIMES to NOT SAY "I'M SORRY." (SORRY.)

Yes, this is another expression like "How are you doing?" It's the best thing to say . . . sometimes. Life is fickle, and unfortunately, we don't always know that saying "I'm sorry" is appropriate. If we have expressed our condolences to someone who says they are "just fine," recoiling at our "pity," it can make us feel embarrassed. It's not a tremendous problem when it happens, but one way out of it is to go back to the principle that "you never really know how someone feels" and just ask a person how they're doing with the experience.

SEEING IT in ACTION:

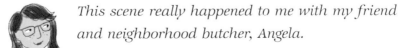

This scene really happened to me with my friend and neighborhood butcher, Angela.

KELSEY Says:

Hi, Angela, how's it going?

Well, Josephine and I are getting divorced.

Wow, I am so sorry. That must be really difficult.

Here, Angela has a couple of options:

Say "That's okay. I am actually quite happy about it." (Which is what she did say in real life.)

(And in real life, I responded, awkwardly: "I am sorry I said I am sorry.")

Or Angela can just say "Thanks" and not acknowledge how she really feels.

To help Angela describe her true feelings, instead of saying "I'm sorry" I could have asked something like "How's that going for you?" and open myself up to actually listen.

Since embarking on this work, I have become a lot less quick to offer condolences, and a lot more ready to ask someone how they are feeling about their news. I'm often surprised at the answers. Friends who feel "optimistic" about a cancer diagnosis, or a person who is hopeful about their divorce. In many of these instances, I would have simply said "I'm sorry." I now ask

"What's that like for you?" or variants like "How's that going?" or "How do you feel about it?" If I intuit it's not feeling good, I might say "That *can* be hard . . ." to give room to describe it that way if it is, but without presuming it's hard for that particular person, who might say that for them it isn't. Asking takes a couple of times of self-conscious effort, but once you see how easy it is, and how well it works for getting to hear other people's experience, which is always far more interesting than what you imagined, you'll begin to do it effortlessly.

HEY, LISTEN:

Sometimes responses to our condolence, like "Thanks, but I'm okay!" or "Why, you didn't cause it!" can make us feel like we made a big empathy misstep and might also make us gun-shy about offering condolences in the future. If someone responds that they're okay, that doesn't actually mean they don't appreciate the spirit of your condolence. It just means you opened up an opportunity for them to say how they're really feeling about it, and they may very well appreciate that, even if they say they're fine. If someone does seem hostile about your overture, that response is really about where they're at emotionally with their situation and very likely has nothing to do with you.

ALLOW FOR SOME IRRATIONALITY.

When your friend's life turns upside down, it's not uncommon that they will act a little nuts. But what about someone going totally crazy? If you have a friend who is doing things that are truly dangerous (or potentially disastrous) to him- or herself or others, then definitely get some advice from other people, including professionals.

It's important to know, however, the difference between something truly destructive and good old-fashioned irrational decision making. The latter is often a normal part of the pain process.

Responses like "You deserve it!" and "I'll tell you when I'm worried about it" can be supportive in helping your friend feel entitled to a dose of exuberant self-care when she needs it.

A periodic check-in, or follow-up, does come in handy to see if someone's "normal" irrational behavior is bordering on something to really worry about. If you're at all concerned, don't be afraid to seek the advice of other people who know what's going on. Remember, you're a kind and caring friend, not a trained professional (unless you really are).

"THIS HAPPENED to ME, Too."

Bad times can make us feel alone and even ashamed. Knowing that someone we admire has gone through something similar can make us feel less alone; less like a singular, personal failure; and even hopeful that, like this person, we can survive this situation too.

Like we wrote about earlier in this chapter, however, remember: just because you have experienced the same thing as someone else does *not* mean you know how they feel. People don't need you to share their exact same feelings down to the molecular level. They just want to know you have been through something similar, and they're not alone.

John lost a parent to suicide, a situation Sandy had experienced in her own life.

I am so sorry to hear about your father's suicide. My mother took her own life five years ago . . .

SANDY

Sandy has a few options to complete her end of the conversation:

1. Tell John more about her experience.

2. Ask John about his experience.

3. Say "I'm sorry. I am here if you need to talk."

John might take comfort in knowing Sandy has had a similar experience, but Sandy should exercise the following guidelines:

- **SHARE HER PERSONAL STORY ONLY IF the PERSON IS NOT IN CRISIS.**
- **MAKE SURE the PERSON in CRISIS GETS to SHARE HIS PERSONAL STORY.**
- **MAKE SURE SHE is ONLY DOING 10% OF THE TALKING, and THEN REDIRECT BACK to JOHN, SO SHE DOESN'T SHARE MORE ABOUT HER EXPERIENCE UNLESS SHE'S ASKED.** (AND EVEN IF ASKED, SHE KEEPS IT SHORT AND SWEET, AND REDIRECTS BACK YET AGAIN TO JOHN.)

"I HAVE FAITH in YOU."

There is nothing quite so daunting as the steep learning curve that comes with life's most critical times. Whether it's loss, illness, infertility, or divorce, there are often a ton of medical, financial, and legal decisions to make that have us feeling profoundly ill-equipped and incompetent. Equally true, there is nothing like the insecurity of being forced into, or opting to take on a new, different life that comes with major change like divorce, job transition, loss, or having a child with special health needs— because all these factors cause us to fear a loss of community, identity, economic security, and our general capacity to cope. That's why, in these times, it's really important to express your faith in a person's ability to manage their situation.

EVEN IF YOU FEEL or UNDERSTAND THEIR FEARS, IF YOU BELIEVE THIS PERSON is OVERALL a COMPETENT, SOUND PERSON WITH GOOD JUDGMENT, **NOW NOW NOW** is THE TIME to LET THEM KNOW THAT. One woman who was contemplating divorce said what supportive words helped her most were: "My friend said that she trusted I would know what was the best course of action."

EMILY Says:

My father-in-law recently died at home of lung cancer, just a few months after his diagnosis. I flew up to visit with the intention of saying good-bye to him and staying for a week to help my mother-in-law with errands and organizing. However, he went downhill very quickly after I arrived, and my mother-in-law and I were thrown into the roles of around-the-clock caregiving for what would be the last two weeks of his life. I'd never been in that situation, and I definitely didn't know what I was doing.

A few days before he died, one of his family members, who I'd never met before, came in for a visit. Before she left, she said to me with a laugh, "You know, you might be the most competent person I've ever met in my life." (LOL.) In that moment, I'd been feeling pretty far from competent, and her confidence in my ability to handle the situation was an invaluable boost when I really needed it.

Maria, an attorney who has been stably employed with the government for ten years, just quit her job and is talking to her sister, Michele.

MARIA

I can't believe I did this. What if I can't find something else instead?

MICHELE

Why did you quit your job? It's a pretty tough market.

MARIA

I don't know. I am such an idiot!

Maria doesn't have a history of quitting jobs and is someone Michele has always admired for her tenacity and maturity. But that doesn't stop Michele from questioning Maria's judgment and making Maria feel insecure about handling a tough job search. Michele's fears for Maria may be rational, but the point is they don't help and only burden her with more doubt.

Let's try this again:

MICHELE

I can imagine it's scary [Here, Michele validates Maria's fears], but I trust your judgment, and I'm confident you will find a new job with a better fit. [Here, she emboldens Maria with confidence based on what she knows about Maria to be true.] Is there anything I can do to help? Like read your résumé or pass it on to folks? [Here, she is offering concrete, tangible help.]

FOCUS on SOMEONE'S FEELINGS, NOT JUST THE FACTS.

When you see someone after their first encounter with an ex, it's natural to want to lead with "Is he dating anyone?" But drilling for the facts without finding out how the person is feeling about them can be a diversion away from the emotional hard stuff. (This is a good example of fact-finding listening, from page 99.) So instead, try asking, *"How did it feel or how was it* to see him after so much time has passed?" A woman with infertility described it like this: "Everyone kept asking me about the medical process. No one seemed to get that I was hurting inside."

Millicent just had a doctor's appointment, in which she learned more about why she's not getting pregnant. She is sharing the news with her sister Deirdre.

MILLICENT

Just got back from the doctor. It turns out there's an issue.

DEIRDRE

What is it?

MILLICENT

They say I'm going through early menopause.

DEIRDRE

What does that mean?

MILLICENT

[explains the details]

DEIRDRE

Wow. How does that happen?

MILLICENT

[tries to explain with limited knowledge]

DEIRDRE

Have you considered a second opinion?

BREAKDOWN: Deirdre has learned some of the facts, but she doesn't know how Millicent feels about them, which is at the heart of support in difficult times. To be even more supportive, Deirdre can take the opportunity to practice empathic listening, establish some emotional resonance, and hear how Millicent is doing with the news.

DEIRDRE

So what does that mean for getting pregnant?

MILLICENT

[Millicent explains.]

DEIRDRE

Wow. How are you feeling? [Here, Deirdre is giving Millicent an opportunity to reflect on the true impact of the news, which has to do with Millicent's hopes for having a baby. This gives Millicent a chance to share her feelings and receive support.]

MILLICENT

I don't know. I feel kind of stunned. Hopeless, really. [Millicent describes more here.]

HOPEFUL STORIES: HELPFUL, most OF THE TIME

Obviously, a terrifying factor for someone going through a hard time is the fear of the unknown. If someone is sick, for example, we just don't know what's going to happen. The situation is beyond our control, which is hard for any human being. It's natural to want to help out your friend by giving them hope. There's a fine line, though, between helping someone feel less daunted, and belittling their very real, warranted fear and anger with "You'll be fine!"

Kelsey is a pessimist by nature, and positive stories can make her queasy. Yet when she got breast cancer, she actually found that she *liked* hopeful stories about situations like hers. As did Emily. It was reassuring to hear real stories of people who had suffered the same diagnosis and survived.

But it's a complicated subject.

MAKE SURE YOUR HOPEFUL STORY IS REAL and ACTUALLY HAPPENED to SOMEONE YOU KNOW. A THING YOU READ ON THE INTERNET DOESN'T COUNT. That said, well-founded stories of hope can be incredibly helpful. If you have your own, or somebody else's positive story about a difficult time (and it *truly* relates!), then by all means, share it. Here are some examples.

INSTEAD OF THIS	TRY THIS
"You will get pregnant!"	*"My friend got pregnant on her third try with IVF."*
"There are other fish in the sea!"	*"You are an amazing, beautiful person and you deserve someone as awesome as you are."*
"Samantha on that show Sex and the City *ran her first marathon while on chemo!"*	*"It's a unique experience for everyone. My sister was able to keep working through most of it, and that's my hope for you."*
"A divorce is not a big deal. Everyone gets divorced these days. Don't worry about it."	*"For what it's worth, I was really surprised by my parents' understanding. But every situation is unique."*
"If you eat unprocessed food and get enough rest, your body will know what to do."	*"My friend had three miscarriages, and her fourth pregnancy is now a walking toddler."*

"I CARE, I LOVE YOU"

Remember how burdensome and unlovable a person in need can feel? There's nothing like being in a shitty or scary time and hearing from others that they love you. In person, via text or email, written on a cake, however and how often you can do it, say I love, admire, respect you, or express whatever kind of adoration you actually have for a person. It can't go wrong. And it's sorely needed, and deeply appreciated.

LIST OF GO-TO PHRASES

KEEP THESE *in* YOUR BACK POCKET
FOR WHENEVER YOU NEED THEM:

- DO YOU WANT *to* TALK ABOUT IT?

- IT'S NOT BORING, I WANT *to* HEAR.

- WHAT'S THAT LIKE FOR YOU?

- HOW ARE YOU DOING, NOW?

- THIS MUST BE HARD, BUT YOU'RE DOING GREAT.

- I TRUST YOU *to* DO THE RIGHT THING.

- I'VE SEEN YOU GET THROUGH HARD THINGS BEFORE. HARD *as* THIS FEELS NOW, I KNOW YOU CAN GET THROUGH THIS.

- YES, KNOWING THIS DOES CHANGE HOW I FEEL ABOUT YOU. I SEE YOU *as* EVEN MORE BEAUTIFUL *and* COURAGEOUS.

- I RESPECT YOU.

- I LOVE YOU.

HEY, LISTEN:

Research shows that talking about our feelings is often easier with friends than with family members. So if you are frustrated that your sibling or parent is not able to listen and talk with you about how you're feeling, you are not alone. It's completely normal for family members to fall down on the job in the feelings realm. It's also true that family members are more likely to pitch in with nitty-gritty help like cleaning, or financial help, so if it feels right (and in some relationships it doesn't), ask them to roll up their sleeves and help—and process your innermost feelings with friends.

QUESTIONS OF ETIQUETTE

IS THIS the RIGHT TIME to TALK?

Where and when matters when it comes to talking. With that in mind, try not to ask someone how they're doing unless you're ready to hear a real answer. For example, don't ask the question as you're exiting the elevator, when the person you're talking to isn't. Also not a good idea: asking when you're within earshot of people not connected to the conversation. As one newly divorced woman said, "First of all, don't bring it up in front of a group of people. If you are really asking out of real concern, do it discreetly."

If you want to connect, to find the right time, you can always ask: "When is a good time to connect?" or just make an overture for lunch or coffee. Or just send an email, note, or card. Don't think that you need to be available at the drop of a hat for any kind of emotionally intense conversation. Unless the person you're asking is in trauma mode or shock, you'll probably win points for thoughtfulness and discretion.

AM I READY to HEAR a REAL ANSWER?

We all have different capacities for listening, and we all lead busy lives. The good news is that you don't have to be your neighbor's armchair therapist unless you really want to be. ONLY ASK "HOW ARE YOU?" IF YOU REALLY HAVE the TIME and a SERIOUS INCLINATION to KNOW. And it's okay if you don't have the time or the inclination. No one wants to share their vulnerability with everyone in any case, and if, ultimately, you're not really *that* interested, or you just don't know a person that well, stick with "I'm sorry." It still shows that you authentically care, and you won't be running the risk of implying more concern than is there.

IS THERE an EXPIRATION DATE on REACHING OUT?

It's common to think that the moment to reach out and acknowledge someone's situation has passed us by. It is almost always okay to reach out a few weeks, months, or in some situations, years after the fact. If something truly bad has happened, a person's life has changed forever, and just because time has passed, they probably haven't stopped thinking about their grief, about the illness they went through, about their ex . . . What's more, many of their friends *will* stop thinking about it as time goes on. People often wind up feeling very alone with the long-term effects of what they went through. Being the person who remembers, even months or years later, isn't a bad thing to be.

LOSS DOESN'T HAVE an EXPIRATION DATE.

One man told us: "After a month or so, no one ever spoke of my mother in any fashion, as though she completely disappeared. Not just that she died, but that she was erased."

SO, WHENEVER YOU FIND OUT SOMETHING BAD HAS HAPPENED to SOMEONE YOU KNOW, FEEL FREE to WRITE, SAY, or DO SOMETHING OUT OF THE BLUE to EXPRESS YOUR CONCERN. BE an UNEXPECTED GIFT. IF YOU'VE ALREADY REACHED OUT ONCE. and YOU CARE to DO SO AGAIN, THAT'S GREAT. IT NEVER GETS OLD.

And if you don't know how someone is feeling about their situation so long after the fact, just say "I don't know how you are doing now, but I heard the news and I'm sorry."

EMPATHY TIP: Saying "I wished I had reached out sooner" is plenty. Spare the person on the receiving end all the reasons/excuses for why you didn't reach out. It doesn't mean the reasons are not valid, but it just doesn't matter that much, and it can make the overture seem more about you than you probably intend.

AM I BEATING a DEAD HORSE?

We may feel we've covered enough ground by asking someone just once about their difficult time, but if your relationship with the person in pain can bear it, it's good to ask again. It's almost always appreciated when we follow up and ask how someone is doing a few weeks or months after their initial time of difficulty. You can even ask "How are you doing with [your situation], now?"

KELSEY Says: *I never expected to feel so much sorrow over my miscarriage for so much time. Four months after it happened, my good friend, Amy, who I see on a regular basis, asked out of the blue how I was doing with it. I was still struggling with it, actually, and until hearing her question, I had felt ashamed for not being over it. Her interest made my grief four months later feel normal and important. The talking about it lasted no more than fifteen seconds. But the impact of her well-timed concern remains to this day.*

A parent whose three-year-old child was diagnosed with cancer said:

> *"Now that we have 'finished treatment' there seems to be the feeling that it is all over, but we have to deal day to day with the worries of recurrent disease, and the lifelong side effects of high-dose chemotherapy. I also felt that my son has missed out on half of his childhood. I want to talk about the trauma we went through, and the aftermath, but no one is asking."*

DON'T BE AFRAID to ASK ABOUT SOMEONE'S CONDITION MORE THAN ONCE. FOLLOW UP.

EMPATHY TIP: The best way to figure out how much or how often to bring up someone's difficult time is by reading their cues. If you ask someone about their issue twice in a conversation, and it's a nonstarter, then that's your cue: don't ask about it any more right then. (If the person broaches the subject on their own, then of course, ask about it with a follow-up question or two.) And if you don't know each other well, there's no need to ask about it more than once.

Many people come to feel self-conscious if their difficult time becomes a perennial source of conversation. If you see someone fairly regularly, whether every day at the office, every few days with your exercise group, or every week for your Sabbath service, it's probably best to *not* check in about your friend's issue every time you see them.

IS SENDING an EMAIL JUST TACKY?

No! Email makes sending love a lot easier, and when something is easier, it is more likely to happen. Despite how embarrassing it can be to resort to the easy option when someone is having the worst possible time, it's so much better than doing nothing. Which means that email is a great option.

EMPATHY TIP: As one woman wrote about receiving emails after her father's death:

"After I sent a mass email to my network of friends, family, and coworkers announcing that my dad had passed, I got tons of messages back. A number of them were from people who cared, but who would not ordinarily take the time to send a card. While some might think it uncool to send a condolence message by email, I really appreciated hearing from folks, regardless of how they reached out."

TEXTING and SOCIAL MEDIA DO COUNT.

Who knew texting could be so powerful a tool for helping people feel better? (Sorry, parents of teenagers everywhere.) Texting isn't just for letting your friends know you're running late (again) or breaking up with someone in the sketchiest possible way. Texting is actually being studied as an effective way for psychologists to support people who are depressed. You may feel that writing fifteen words or fewer on social media or text, or sending an emoji of a glass of wine, isn't the right way to connect with someone when they're in pain. But remember—it's not about finding the "right words," but simply connecting. Sometimes, we only need to know people are thinking about us and don't need to always talk about what we are feeling. So if you are hovering over your computer or phone, wondering whether to email or post a condolence or just say "hi," "love you," or share something else, the answer is yes. A call is an additional bonus if you are a close friend. But virtual comfort really does count.

IS CALLING EVEN APPROPRIATE ANYMORE?

With all the other ways to communicate at our fingertips, people rarely get on the phone anymore. When the phone rings, it can feel intrusive, especially if it's a number we don't recognize. So do you call someone when they're in crisis? If you are not already very close friends, we recommend you don't pick up the phone. If you aren't close, *definitely* do not call within days of a tragic event or difficult news. A card or an email is better.

However, if you *are* good friends or close family, *call!* The person can always choose to not pick up. One of the women Kelsey surveyed commented:

> *"I would have liked more phone calls from a few close*
> *friends after I lost my husband. I don't expect them*
> *to know exactly what to say or really be able to help,*
> *but just a simple check-in, a phone call or message,*
> *would have let me know they were thinking of me.*
> *That would have been really supportive and helpful."*

EMPATHY TIP: Avoid expressions like "I've left you a couple of messages." One of the worst things you can do is make someone feel pressure to call back. Much better to simply say "No need to call back" and leave it at that.

ALL THAT SAID: SEND a CARD!

Given that so much of our modern communications are via electronics, getting an actual card—you know, one made out of paper that comes in an envelope with a stamp on the outside and everything—feels, these days, even more like someone made a special effort. Unlike a text or a tweet, you can display a card as a reminder that someone was thinking of you. Many of us keep cards for years, if not for a lifetime, reading them with every move of our stuff. And, even better, if you're struggling with what to say, cards can do a great job of helping you find the right words.

If you can find the time to send a card, please do. Embrace the challenge of buying a stamp—remember those?—and finding a person's physical address! Where there's a will, there's a way.

EMPATHY TIP: In an ideal world, you wouldn't ask a grieving person for their address. You can resort to asking for it if you must—it's not a huge deal— but first, try and find it some other way.

SOMETIMES, PEOPLE NEED SPACE.

We've written a lot here about reaching out, so it goes against our very instincts to state it, but sometimes a person just wants to forget about their situation or feel normal again. In these times, if you don't think they are in a dangerous situation, you can respect a person's wish to be alone. Or offer to go to a movie or have some other kind of night out. For those times when someone is too tired for entertainment or chatting, simple company is great. As one woman who was ill described: "I didn't want to talk. I was too tired. But my friend came by and hung out on the couch and read while I stayed in bed. It helped me feel less lonely."

OKAY, I'LL TELL YOU ABOUT MY BORING LIFE.

There's nothing like seeing your neighbor in mourning or friend bald from chemotherapy to make you feel a tad sheepish when complaining about your boss. There are certainly times to leave your own worries at the door and focus on your friend. What people in a difficult time often fear, however, is that their scary, awful situation means they are left out of other people's lives. Yes, not being able to find jeans that fit your waistline is a "good problem" to have, but it just might be your problem today. If your friend or neighbor or colleague isn't in crisis or emotionally distraught, then just be who you are and share your situation. Because people in grief want to feel like you see them as a whole person, not just a griever, or a patient.

One young man, Kevin, who lost both his parents in a plane crash put it this way:

> *"I felt best when people didn't treat me differently even after they learned of my loss. I returned home after spending a month at my parents' house, and some friends gave me a low-key dinner party when I returned. It helped me ease back into a life that I knew would never be the same."*

BOTTOM LINE:

KNOWING WHEN to LISTEN and WHAT to SAY
STARTS WITH:

- SAYING "I'M SORRY."

- ASKING "HOW ARE YOU, TODAY?" (Don't forget to listen to the answer.)

- FOCUSING ON and ACKNOWLEDGING the PERSON'S PRESENT FEELINGS, NOT JUST the FACTS.

- PAYING ATTENTION to CUES: IS IT a GOOD TIME? OR DOES the PERSON NEED a LITTLE SPACE? (DON'T BE AFRAID to FOLLOW UP IF NOW ISN'T the RIGHT TIME.)

- EXPRESSING THAT the PERSON IS NOT ALONE.

- EXPRESSING FAITH in the PERSON'S (PROBABLY RATTLED) JUDGMENT.

- SHARING the LOVE.

- USING TECHNOLOGY FOR GOOD.

- GIVING SPACE WHEN SPACE is NEEDED.

- BEING YOURSELF WITH YOUR "MUNDANE" PROBLEMS.

CHAPTER 5:
SMALL GESTURES
make a BIG DIFFERENCE

> "I loved her texts. Just knowing that she noticed,
> and cared, was all that I needed; it's not like she
> had a magic lever that would release balloons
> from the ceiling and make my disease go away."
> —Ken, diagnosed with MS

One day, Boris was at the deli when he spotted Noboru (at least, he was pretty sure his name was Noboru). They had been part of the same cycling crew back in the day, and Boris had always liked him. Boris was about to say hi when he remembered he'd heard Noboru's father had recently passed away.

He was struck with doubt. Just by looking at him across the store, Boris could see that Noboru wasn't in great shape, but he didn't know what to do. Too embarrassed to say anything, Boris paid in cash so he could get out of there faster and not have to face him.

But Boris didn't get away clean. For the rest of the day, he couldn't get Noboru's face out of his mind, so that night, he looked up his email and wrote him:

> *I saw you at the store today but was too chicken*
> *to say anything. I'm really sorry about your loss.*
> *I can't imagine what that is like. I'm really sorry.*

Boris pressed send before he could back out.

The next morning, there was no reply from Noboru, so he wondered if his email was inappropriate. But that afternoon, Noboru responded:

> *Hey. It has been horrible. Worse than you*
> *can imagine. But your email really helped*
> *me out today. Really. Thanks.*

Boris wasn't proud of running out of the deli, but he felt really glad he sent that note. And it was actually a lot easier to do than he thought.

Sometimes, what's holding us back from offering comfort isn't that we don't care enough, but that we don't feel we have the time or the bandwidth to do something that will make a difference. We may feel that we have to be 100 percent available all the time when we're around someone in a tough situation. It's not unreasonable to think that saying "I'm sorry" is an inadequate response to, say, the loss of a loved one. Or that asking "How are you?" and genuinely wanting to know means we are then responsible for talking with this person about their situation until the end of time.

THE GOOD NEWS is, THESE FEARS are NORMAL.
THE BETTER NEWS is, THESE FEARS are NOT RATIONAL.

WE'LL EXPLAIN EXACTLY WHY WITH OUR
THIRD TOUCHSTONE of SHOWING UP:
SMALL GESTURES
MAKE A
BIG DIFFERENCE.

TINY PEBBLES MAKE WIDE RIPPLES.

In Kelsey's Empathy Bootcamp workshops, participants put together what they call a Gesture Wall, a convincing demonstration of the massive comforting power of small gestures. To create the Gesture Wall, each person writes down one thing, a gesture, that a neighbor, friend, colleague, or someone they barely know did for them that made a big difference in their lives when times were dark. These are then posted on a wall and reviewed in total by all the workshop participants. The takeaway is always the same: the gestures themselves are often very small and require little effort, but the effect they have on the receivers is significant, sometimes even years later.

Equally valuable about the exercise is what it reveals about the variety of people who matter in our lives. They include neighbors, colleagues, good friends, strangers, and family. The biggest revelation for viewers of the Gesture Wall is that for most situations, comforting someone is not a Herculean effort, because providing support is not the sole responsibility of any one person. And that's because:

CARING TAKES a VILLAGE.

You are not a soul doctor. When someone is in a rough time, you are not being called upon to commit the next twenty years to helping them work through every problem they'll ever have. People who can drop everything and care for us are a wonderful gift, but that person doesn't have to be you. If you feel overwhelmed by life and are maxed for time or emotional bandwidth—but you also care—take this to heart: offering comfort is *not* leading someone on, or committing yourself to offering more comfort later. It can be a onetime offer; you can decide how much to give. IT'S PERFECTLY OKAY *if* WHAT YOU OFFER *is* SIMPLE OR SEEMINGLY SMALL.

EMPATHY WARM-UP: CREATING a GESTURE WALL

It can be hard to believe that others will find your small gifts valuable, and the following exercise can help. Answer the following brief questions for yourself, and then maybe ask them of two friends (you can even do your own miniversion of Empathy Bootcamp, where you all write your answer(s) to each question on sticky notes, and when you're done, stick them up on the wall and spend some time looking at the range of responses):

1. What's something a colleague did that meant a lot to me in a difficult time?

2. What's something an acquaintance did for me that comforted or helped me?

3. What's something an old friend I hadn't seen in forever did for me?

4. What did a good friend or family do that supported me?

5. What were some of the most amazing gifts I received in my difficult time?

After considering the range of your own responses (and/or those of your friends), check out the following examples of gestures collected from Kelsey's workshops. Some of these might just give you an idea of something you can do to help someone right now.

While you look at these example responses collected from Empathy Bootcamps, think back to the state of being a grieving, freaked-out person. Consider how these gestures, in their small, cumulative ways, help with the following: loneliness, shame, fear, overwhelm, uncertainty, and financial insecurity.

FROM COLLEAGUES

MY STUDENTS SENT ME A HUGE BASKET OF ORGANIC, HEALTHY FOOD.

OFFERED to DONATE PAID TIME OFF WHEN I WAS CLOSE to RUNNING OUT.

MY BOSS LET ME WORK FROM HOME.

STOPPED BY MY DESK TO SAY HELLO.

THE OFFICE STAFF SENT ME FLOWERS.

WHEN I WOKE UP FROM SURGERY, MY COLLEAGUES HAD DECORATED MY HOSPITAL WALLS WITH HEALING WORDS, QUOTES, and PHRASES THAT WERE MEANINGFUL to ME.

MADE a GIANT CARD at WORK FOR PEOPLE to WRITE COMMENTS ON.

SOMEONE I ONLY KNOW FROM WORK SENT ME a $150 FOOD GIFT CERTIFICATE WHILE I WAS RECOVERING, ASKING THAT I FOCUS ON NOURISHING MYSELF.

FROM NEIGHBORS/ACQUAINTANCES

LEFT FLOWERS and FOOD OUTSIDE OUR DOOR WHEN WE GOT BACK FROM the HOSPITAL.

HEARING FROM PEOPLE WHO HAD LOST SOMEBODY to SUICIDE WAS INCREDIBLY POWERFUL.

AN ANONYMOUS NEIGHBOR LEFT A BOX OF DIAPERS on MY STEPS WITH a NOTE THAT SIMPLY SAID "YOU GOT THIS!"

OUR NEIGHBORS MADE US MEALS AFTER OUR BABY WAS BORN.

TEXTED or CALLED to CHECK IN.

OUR LANDLORD DELIVERED BOXES OF SNACKS and SOFT DRINKS WHEN MY HUSBAND WAS RECUPERATING.

OUR NEIGHBORS HANDLED ALTERNATE-SIDE-OF-THE-STREET PARKING OF OUR CAR FOR a COUPLE OF WEEKS AFTER MY SURGERY SO WE WOULDN'T HAVE to THINK ABOUT IT.

FROM FRIENDS

MY FRIEND RESEARCHED GRANTS and FUNDING FOR ADULT CANCER SURVIVORS and COMPLETED APPLICATIONS FOR ME.

FRIENDS FROM CHURCH WOULD VISIT OUR SON in a COMA, SO WE COULD GET a BREAK.

MY FRIEND SENT ME a LINK to a RIDICULOUS YouTUBE VIDEO THAT I ENDED UP WATCHING WHENEVER I NEEDED a BOOST.

CHECKED in and SUPPORTED MY PARTNER WHEN I WAS SICK. IT FELT SO COMFORTING to KNOW SHE WAS GETTING SUPPORT, LOVE and TENDING WHEN I COULDN'T DO IT.

MY FRIEND GIFTED ME an ACUPUNCTURE SESSION AFTER a TERRIBLE BREAKUP.

SENT ME a CARD EVERY OTHER WEEK, WITH SILLY STICKERS, THOUGHTFUL QUOTES, and OVERALL NICE MESSAGES OF "HELLO, I'M THINKING OF YOU."

I WAS EMOTIONALLY DEVASTATED SINCE MY DIVORCE. MY FRIEND JUST STARTED CASUALLY CLEANING the KITCHEN COUNTER as I TALKED ABOUT MY PROBLEMS. I FELT CARED FOR in a GENTLE and UNASSUMING WAY.

FROM FAMILY

MY SISTER CAME BY and CLEANED OUR HOUSE FOR US. SHE ISN'T a VERY EMOTIONAL PERSON and THIS WAS a WAY FOR HER to HELP. I REALLY APPRECIATED the EFFORT.

MY AUNT TOOK ME OUT FOR COFFEE EVERY TUESDAY to GET ME OUT OF the HOUSE.

MY BROTHER GOT OUR CAR CLEANED and FILLED IT WITH GAS.

MY SISTER PUT HER ORGANIZATIONAL SKILLS to GOOD USE and ORGANIZED OUR KITCHEN CABINETS WHILE MY WIFE WAS UNDERGOING CHEMO.

DID MY LAUNDRY.

MY COUSIN VOLUNTEERED to BE "FAMILY COMMUNICATOR" and SENT OUT a WEEKLY EMAIL to OUR FAMILY UPDATING EVERYONE on MY CONDITION.

FROM STRANGERS

WHEN a STRANGER WOULD APPROACH ME and WARMLY ASK, "ARE YOU OKAY?"

I WAS on the GROUND, LEANING AGAINST the GLASS of the AIRPORT TERMINAL WINDOW, CRYING MY EYES OUT. A STRANGER CAME UP and ASKED IF I WAS OKAY. I SAID YES, WHICH WASN'T TRUE. I DIDN'T WANT to TALK to HER ABOUT IT. BUT I WAS REALLY TOUCHED THAT SHE REACHED OUT. SHE MADE ME FEEL BETTER.

THINK ABOUT THIS:
"FEAR-BUSTING" QUESTIONS

1. How many of the gestures you just read took a lot of time, energy, or money?

2. How many of them were dependent on having an impressive grasp of human psychology?

3. Is there any one thing someone did that "cured" somebody of pain?

4. Were the gestures by acquaintances, colleagues, or even friends intrusive?

5. Did the helpers need to know specific details of the situation in order to help?

EMPATHY TIP: Flowers are awesome, and, as cliché as they may be, they really do wonders for brightening up someone's day. But overt gestures and gifts in public spaces, like the workplace, may prompt questions from coworkers, inadvertently making the network of people in the know wider than is desired. In which case, discreetly leave something else (Donuts! Chocolate! HBO Go password!).

YOUR EMPATHY SWEET SPOT

Once we've decided to support someone, our natural first question is usually: "Well, what do they need?" This is a totally logical question when you're faced with fixing a faucet or a car. (And someday Emily hopes to become a person capable of doing at least one of those things.) But counterintuitively, thinking about what someone in a difficult time might need is a less helpful strategy when trying to support them. Instead, you can narrow down the parameters of care to something very manageable and even fun to do, by asking yourself: **WHAT CAN I GIVE?**

YOUR AUTHENTIC GIFT STARTS WITH WHAT YOU CAN GIVE, NOT WITH WHAT SOMEONE NEEDS.

If you care, doing something is important. But doing something you *like* to do, and not something you would normally *resist* doing, is invaluable.

THAT'S BECAUSE DOING SOMETHING WE NATURALLY LIKE to DO MEANS WE'RE MORE LIKELY to DO IT.

Nobody sucks at empathy. Just like laughing, we were all born with the ability to show we care. You just might need a little help to figure out what you're good at. And while you're probably not good at *everything*, we know you're good at *something*, and you can use that something to be supportive. You can find the thing you love to give and know you can give well and offer up that very specific gesture.

To give you a concrete idea of what we're talking about, take a look at our Empathy Menu that was inspired by Kelsey's friend Meaghan, a young cancer survivor who describes in a personal essay the roles people played during her chemotherapy treatment, naming them "an extension of my immune system." Before you review the menu, just remember: not every difficult time requires everything on this list. Furthermore, no one is good at everything on this list. (If you are, we would like to meet you and be friends with you in case we require your support in the future.)

The EMPATHY MENU

Is good at asking questions, is attentive to the answers, and offers up space for the person to just be quiet with someone, if talking feels like too much.

the OPPOSABLE-THUMBED

Sends texts just saying *Hi* and *I'm thinking of you.*

the SPIRITUAL

Prays and sends positive, healing intentions.

the POET

Sends a card, notes to say *Hello*, *I'm thinking of you*, *I'm sorry*, *I'm proud*, or *You are awesome*. Or something else even more poetic.

the PRACTICAL GIFT-GIVER

Gives coupons for a cleaning service, food, massages.

the CHEF

Drops off fresh and/or frozen meals.

the WHIMSICAL/ FUNNY GIFT-GIVER

Gives silly gifts like a voodoo doll or a bright pink wig, maybe takes the person to a stand-up show.

the PERSEVERER

Forgives broken plans and keeps on scheduling. (This is actually a characteristic everyone should aspire to when helping.)

the CHAUFFEUR Drives and keeps company on important dates.

the CRAFTER Makes something unique and meaningful—a quilt, a song, an awesome playlist.

the NETWORKER Finds out people who can help and makes an introduction, from medical and alternative doctors, to lawyers, to therapists, to someone else who's been in a similar situation.

the ENTERTAINER Invites the person out to movies, drinks, or accompanies them in a marathon of watching the dumbest reality television they can find.

the RESEARCHER Digs into the latest research (possibly shielding the patient from falling into the vast and terrifying abyss of medical information on the Internet).

the GARDENER Does the yard work, brings plants.

the WORKHORSE   Runs errands—from food shopping, to picking up dry cleaning, to housework.

the ORGANIZER   Creates binders of important financial, health, and legal information.

the BABYSITTER/ EXTENDED CAREGIVER   Spends time with the kids or the frail people in our lives.

the PROJECT MANAGER   Coordinates other people's help. (Nobody wants eight casseroles on the same day.)

the FINANCIER   Helps out with costs on babysitting, medical or legal bills, and so on, and doesn't need to be paid back.

the PUBLIC RELATIONS GURU   The point of contact for sharing updates with friends.

the HOST(ESS)   Invites the person to stay at their house or invites them over for meals.

If you'd rather lick a live wire than talk about something emotionally difficult, but you really DO care, there's *huge* relief in the Empathy Menu for you. It's good to know you can leave flowers at the door and run, or pen a condolence card, or sweep up your bereaved neighbor's yard without having to talk about his wife's passing in a way that makes you feel awkward. By helping or reaching out in some small way, you've acknowledged what someone is going through, and it will really make a difference in their day. And if that's all you feel you're capable of, that's *fine*. And the more "fine" you feel in giving what you can give, the more likely you will be to give it, give it more often, and who knows—when you do have time or bandwidth—even give more. But the point is to give what you can give and feel good about giving.

So if you hate having emotional conversations, but really love to garden, then offer up that skill to someone who needs it, even doing it while they aren't home, if that's what makes you more comfortable. If, on the other hand, you can't be counted on to do chores for anyone else, because you can't even count on getting them done for yourself, but you're a great listener, then trust that by just asking someone how they are doing, when you really have the inclination and time to know, is really valuable.

EMPATHY WORKOUT: WHAT are YOUR EMPATHY SUPERPOWERS?

Choose two things you're good at, and two you know you can cross off the list right away. For example:

KELSEY Says:

I enjoy buying flowers, and even hosting people for a long spell, which is something a lot of people won't offer to do, so I offer it up fairly regularly. But cleaning? Cooking? Not my strong suit. I used to feel obligated to cook for people, because it seemed like that's what I was supposed to do. But the stress of it made it hard for me to give with love, and actually made me a bit of a Fretter (see page 76).

EMILY Says:

I really like making things, and given infinite time, I'd love to be embroidering pillows or doing something crafty. But honestly, at this point in my life, it makes more sense for me to send gifts like massages, food-delivery service gift certificates—or there's always a card.

JUST SO YOU KNOW, I AM TOTALLY ON BOARD FOR DRIVING YOU TO TREATMENT, CLEANING YOUR PLACE, HELPING PICK OUT FLATTERING WIGS, COMING UP WITH BAD-ASS VISUALIZATION EXERCISES, AND IF you TWIST MY ARM, I GUESS I'D ALSO BE COOL WITH LYING ON THE COUCH and WATCHING TRASHY TV TOGETHER. I KNOW. IT'S A SACRIFICE I'M WILLING TO MAKE. ♥ ♥ ♥ ♥ ♥ I LOVE YOU. ♥ ♥ ♥ ♥ ♥

When we recognize the comforting value of our unique talents—and even better, accept the limits we have on what we can do—the more likely we are to offer our few, but valued gifts. This is way preferable to having a gesture dragged out of us by a person in crisis. Look at this sample conversation scenario to see what we mean.

CHEN

I'm a mess. I just can't get out of bed.

MEAGHAN

I'm so sorry, Chen. Let me know if there is anything I can do.

CHEN

Uhh . . . Thanks. No, I'm okay.

So Meaghan cares and wants to help. But Chen doesn't really know where to begin with asking for help, so he says he's okay. But he's not really okay. And because he's not okay, he doesn't feel comfortable telling Meaghan what he needs—even if he knows what it is.

Let's try this again:

CHEN

I'm a mess. I just can't get out of bed.

I'm so sorry, Chen. Let me know if there is anything I can do.

MEAGHAN

Thanks, Meaghan. I have to go to the funeral on Tuesday. Can you come feed my cat?

CHEN

Ooh, sorry, I can't. I'm allergic.

MEAGHAN

How about moving my car when I'm gone?

CHEN

Oh, gosh, I don't know how to drive. Anything else?

MEAGHAN

Um, no. Thanks. I'm all set.

CHEN

In that second scenario, Chen was brave to ask, and he took Meaghan at her word. And of course, Meaghan wanted to be helpful. But there was no way for Chen to know what kind of help she really had in mind. Any rational person would do what Chen did and eventually give up.

The easiest way for Meaghan to truly be helpful would be to offer her specific, authentic gift with love and confidence. This could be any of the following:

MEAGHAN

I'm a great gardener and would love to come by and water your plants while you're away. I can also take in the mail.

OR

MEAGHAN

I can't drive (or I'm allergic to cats), but I'll find you someone who can and coordinate it for you. When's your flight? I'll make sure someone will be there to pick you up.

OR

If Meaghan can't or doesn't want to do any chores, she can just say "I'm sorry." If she's a listener, she can offer to listen and say "Wanna tell me what's going on?" And if she's a gift giver, she can leave something to be waiting for Chen when he gets back.

In any of the above scenarios, Meaghan offers what she can and wants to handle and doesn't offer what she can't or doesn't want to do. This will be easier for Meaghan and feels much better to Chen.

If you aren't in a position to offer anything specific to fill a need, but still want to do something, like send a gift, a card, or a poem, go ahead. Again, look at the Empathy Menu. It's likely if you were to email someone asking what they need, they wouldn't have said "A really good playlist for my chemo session." But you are a lover of music and want to create a playlist—then *just do it* and don't wait for someone to ask for it. But wait, you say, you have no time to make an entire playlist? Okay, just post your favorite inspirational song on the person's Facebook page. You see where we're going here, right?

YOUR AUTHENTIC GIFT, WHETHER it's BEING ASKED OF YOU OR NOT, IS STILL REALLY AWESOME to RECEIVE.

WHEN YOUR OFFER ISN'T ACCEPTED

A lot of times, we *do* offer to help, and it isn't accepted. This may be because:

1. The offer isn't specific enough;

2. The need isn't there at that time, but could very well be at some point in the future; or

3. The need was never really there, nor will it ever be.

To solve the first problem, you can just make your offer more specific. For example:

- "On Thursdays, I'm free and can do any kind of errands you might need for two hours."

- "I have a second car I never use; if you need one for out-of-town guests, I'd be happy to loan it."

If a person doesn't accept your offer the first time you make it, you can reoffer a few more times (but no more than that) over several days, or weeks, or months, and see what happens.

HEY, LISTEN:

Your offer may not be needed right now, and that's just fine.

KELSEY Says:

When I went through my breast cancer treatment, one offer—for help with child care for two-year-old Georgia—came three times over three months. Each and every time, my husband, Mike, and I declined, because we hadn't hung out with that family in over a year, and Georgia didn't enjoy being with families she didn't know well. But that we didn't need that child care didn't matter—the mere offer, repeated as it was, gave us a tremendous sense of feeling cared for. The thought really counted because it was an offer of tangible relief.

It may also be the case that you made your gesture and never heard about how it was received. And you know what? Not getting a thank-you note in these situations is completely normal. If you need convincing, consider this: Kelsey's organization, Help Each Other Out, put together public art exhibits on "Being There" in San Francisco and New York that featured portraits of people in a difficult time, along with their stories of a gesture that helped get them through it. The portraits and stories were displayed in neighborhood corridors in store windows that stretched over many blocks. So clearly, these gestures were meaningful. However, more times than not, the people who had done these gestures had never been thanked by the people who were so clearly comforted by them. Because when you are in grief, or freaked out and scared, you often don't write thank-you notes.

EMPATHY TIP: The sick, grieving, or freaked-out person always gets a pass. Always offer up your gift with a "No need to write a thank-you." And mean it.

OFFER YOUR GIFT WITH JOY
(FOR REAL.)

A major, common fear held by those in crisis is that they're becoming a burden. Relieving them of this fear is simple:

- Practice a moment of gratitude that you have this opportunity to be of service to someone in your life.

- Make no mention of any sacrifices (like change in schedule or financial cost) you might have made for this supportive gesture to happen.

- Try to offer what you can before the person even asks for it in a matter-of-fact, happy-to-do-it kind of way. If they ask for your help, respond with saying how it would actually be a pleasure for you to do it (because remember, a person in need fears being a burden). For example: "Not at all, it's no problem . . . Doing somebody else's housework is a good excuse to get me away from the kids"; "I'm going to the store anyway, so what can I get you?"; "Walking the dog will get me outside"; "I've been dying to hang out with your daughter Suzie"; "Oh great, I finally get to try out that new lasagna recipe."

- If something is being asked of you that you can't do, come up with something else on the Empathy Menu that you can do instead. Maybe the person won't need it, but at least they know you are serious about trying to help and may enlist your service in the future.

EMPATHY TIP: We all have moments where we can't follow through or even forget a commitment we made. It happens. But when someone is in their time of difficulty, they are feeling extra sensitive and are depending on you. In these times, when you don't follow through, it hurts. So, do what you can to make your offer happen, and give plenty of notice when you can't.

People might want some kinds of news handled with more discretion than others. Given that we live in the age of social media shares, and our culture is more open than ever about a range of life's hard times, it can be difficult to imagine that someone might not want many people to know what's going on. For some people, and likely with some issues more than others, there are concerns around (1) privacy, (2) fear, and (3) plain old healthy denial. All these factors mean that discretion should always be a consideration.

PRIVACY

Some issues feel more private to people than others:

·INFERTILITY The numerous ups and downs and uncertainties, the private nature of the endeavor, and the judgmental responses this issue often elicits can mean that this experience is not one shared among a wide circle. For people with a really interested, emotionally aware, and inquisitive group of friends, it's possible they may feel others are asking too much about

ONE QUESTION to AVOID: ARE YOU PREGNANT? BECAUSE WHEN SHE WANTS YOU to KNOW, YOU'LL KNOW.

their experience. For others, who never get asked, infertility is incredibly isolating. In general, unless you are very close, don't expect to ask about it, unless she brings it up with you first. If you are close, ask occasionally—not every time you see her—and be really open to cues about whether to press for more information.

•MISCARRIAGE This very painful loss can often be kept private out of choice, when it is too hard to mention the grief out loud. Or because of stigma when women fear judgment about why the miscarriage happened. People can also remain silent about their miscarriage to keep baby-making plans quiet from bosses and colleagues, or from parents who are craving that first grandchild, or anxious friends who want to start buying up little baby hats.

IF SHE TOLD YOU SHE WAS PREGNANT, YOU CAN (AND SHOULD) REACH OUT. BUT OTHERWISE, IT'S NOT CRITICAL to DO SO.

·LOSS OF a JOB There is reputational damage to being fired, and often some significant shame in the perceived rejection. Casually reaching out with news, "I heard you were fired," can cause panic about gossip. *However*, if you want to reach out because you want to tell someone they did a great job, they really need to hear that. Just do so with tact:

"I HEARD YOU AREN'T WORKING FOR _____ ANYMORE. I JUST WANTED to SAY HOW MUCH I ADMIRED THE WORK YOU DID THERE."

·ILLNESS People may keep their illness private so they don't have to deal with other people's reactions, which often involve an unwanted opinion or an emotional response that the sick person feels obligated to manage. If the illness is somewhat chronic, people's feelings can change about how much to disclose; sometimes, they may feel like sharing more than other times. At work, news of an illness might jeopardize a job or chances at a promotion. For some, keeping the news of their illness quiet in the workplace and other social settings helps them feel "normal" without the disease taking over their identity. Look for cues about how someone says they want to handle their situation; often you will notice if they feel fairly public about it, or they'll give some indication that they'd rather keep things quiet.

·DIVORCE Divorce not only impacts a couple, but that couple's circle of family and friends, meaning the news of a split often unleashes a wave of opinions and theories from anyone who's ever met the involved parties. It's not uncommon for those exiting their marriage to want a good handle on their situation before sharing it with others. What's more, some kinds of workplaces and religious groups may frown upon divorce, creating fear about being a source of speculation and gossip until the person feels ready to manage it. If someone is deliberating over decisions and you want to be a close confidant, just listen—and work very hard to not weigh in. If you aren't close, but you have a long-standing relationship, and the news of the divorce has been made public, you can reach out to express your overall admiration for a person in what *might* be a hard time. However, make sure you don't sound like you're fishing for gossip by asking "why" it happened, and be open to hearing how a person is doing with their situation.

·LOSS Of all these issues, death can be the most public. What may be a more private matter is the exact nature of someone's grief—namely, that not all loss comes with pain, that it sometimes comes with relief, or a whole bunch of ambivalent feelings. In general, reaching out to the griever in some way, if you care, is generally appreciated. You may presume there is sorrow attached to their loss, but don't dwell on it unless such sorrow is pronounced. Provide room for the griever to talk openly about how they feel; and if you are not close, a simple "I'm sorry" will do.

IN GENERAL, REACHING OUT *to* THE GRIEVER *in* SOME WAY, IF YOU CARE, IS USUALLY APPRECIATED.

FEAR and OVERWHELM

Finding out that your child has a disability? Hearing the news of your own terrible diagnosis? Unexpectedly discovering that your partner is filing for divorce? All these situations can cause shock, fear, and a sense of being completely overwhelmed, and these feelings are another reason people might want their situation handled discreetly. Just saying out loud that the scary situation is happening can make it more "real" than someone wants it to be.

> "We decided not to share the news beyond my
> husband's immediate family and best friend. A few
> months later, he shared his illness more broadly,
> and there were some who expressed dismay that
> they weren't told sooner. What they didn't seem
> to understand was how hard, scary, and very
> personal it was for the person with a life-threatening
> illness to have to tell others what's going on."
>
> —Valerie, whose husband had cancer

It is not uncommon in these situations for a person to appoint a communications guru (see the Empathy Menu on page 155) who can communicate the details of a particular situation and serve as a kind of project manager, fielding questions and offers of assistance. (So if you're a communications-friendly person, feel free to volunteer that service.)

HEY, LISTEN:

When people share their vulnerability with us, it's a sign of trust and friendship. So it's natural that when a friend presents their difficult news, after figuring it out without you, that you want to ask "Why didn't you tell me?" But in some situations, it's just too hard or scary for the person in a difficult time to talk about it. Instead of focusing on what that person didn't do, focus on how you can be of support now. If your friend has a general pattern of holding back vulnerability and it's hard for you, you can address it at some later time, just not around the time of crisis.

HEALTHY DENIAL

Not everyone chooses to "deal" with their issue by sharing, talking, or processing it.

This may not be your chosen method, but some people find engaging around a devastating issue simply too distracting from their career, their family, their lives.  Author Jackie Collins, who battled stage 4 cancer while still publishing books, said: "I didn't want sympathy. Sympathy can weaken you." You may not agree with this choice, but in most cases, it's not your job to change that.

How to navigate between respecting someone's privacy and simply not showing up? There is no rule, other than the rule of thumb we've both chosen to live by:

IF YOU HAVE to CHOOSE BETWEEN OFFERING TOO MUCH OR TOO LITTLE CARE, WE WOULD CHOOSE TOO MUCH.

That said, pay attention to cues and consider the following:

- Respect it when someone doesn't want to talk about what's going on.

- Ask people in the person's inner circle if they have an inkling of how someone wants the news handled.

- Pay attention to verbal and nonverbal cues, if you can.

- Be aware of how you would want the news handled yourself.

- If you believe privacy is a core concern, yet you feel strongly about reaching out, do so discreetly.

And finally:

If you overstep your concern in one person's case, you have not failed at empathy. You are still great at empathy—it just wasn't what that person wanted right then. It happens to everyone. But in most cases, your efforts at outreach will be appreciated. So take the risk, unless someone explicitly tells you otherwise.

WHEN SHOULD I REACH OUT?

The best time to reach out depends on your relationship to a person, and the nature of the hard time. There is no hard-and-fast rule, but the following are some general guidelines.

If you are very close to the person:

- If the person reached out to you, make contact IMMEDIATELY by phone, and then in person if possible.

- If you've heard the news through someone else, it's best to contact the person by text or email in THE FIRST FEW DAYS. Follow up with a call and leave a voice mail.

- Make sure to visit the person WITHIN THE WEEK, and within a few days if possible.

- When visiting isn't possible, be a REGULAR PRESENCE with texting and phone calls. Just be sure to stress that there's no need to call or text back.

If you are an acquaintance, with, say, regular interaction at work or in your social life:

- YOU CAN WAIT a WEEK OR TWO to send an email, a card, or flowers.

- DON'T MAKE IMMEDIATE CONTACT, as it can overwhelm the person.

- IT'S PROBABLY BEST NOT to CALL, even if you have been in a similar situation. People often feel overwhelmed by too many phone calls.

If you have limited social interaction, for example, you don't know someone's last name but you see them a lot in the neighborhood, at social events, or in the workplace and you have a mutual regard:

- YOU CAN WAIT to acknowledge the issue in person or with a card when you see them next, which may even be several weeks or more. But first, consider the level of discretion that certain experiences might require.

- YOU DON'T HAVE to SAY ANYTHING.

A SPECIAL NOTE to BOSSES

According to research, and also anyone you'd ever ask, "high-quality connections" and compassion in the workplace help employees readjust after significant loss or illness. When bosses don't acknowledge employees' difficult times, it doesn't make the employees more productive; they'll probably be quite the opposite. Instead of pretending everything is normal, simply acknowledge what has happened.

THE MOMENT YOU HEAR OF AN EMPLOYEE'S DIFFICULTY, FIND a PRIVATE MOMENT to SAY "I'M SORRY."

Bosses should also strongly consider sending flowers and/or a card, should follow up with the employee to find out if any special accommodations are needed, and should expect to be flexible as time goes on. Going the extra mile to work with HR and a willingness to get creative around time off is crucial, too. What we've heard time and time again is that the return in employee loyalty is well worth it.

> *"My boss was very flexible about my work schedule and let me work at home for a few months. I was probably a pretty poor worker at that time, but it paid off in the long run. I stayed with the organization for a long time and really gave a lot later."*
>
> —Alvin, whose daughter was born with a heart condition

Also, make sure to ask your employee how the situation is going every once in a while. As a young man with multiple sclerosis told us: "I don't want to focus on my illness in the workplace, but I appreciate that my boss checks in to make sure that I'm okay."

THE BOTTOM LINE: ADEQUATE IS AWESOME.

IF WHAT YOU CAN OR WANT to GIVE IS NOTHING MORE THAN A SIMPLE "I'M SORRY," THAT'S BETTER THAN TURNING AWAY.

If the thing you most love to give isn't needed right now, your offer (even if it's not accepted) is better than turning away. And if what you want to give is the moon and stars because you have that much time, inclination, or sense of responsibility (not to mention resources and a rocket ship), that's better than turning away, too.

If we imagine that helping equals *rescuing* someone from their pain, we're more likely to shy away from the effort. We could easily feel unprepared to handle such a large responsibility or erroneously conclude it's not our place to do so in the first place. Even when we're feeling confident in our ability to shoulder a ton of things for other people, it takes only one long day at work, one awful night with the kids, or one awesome invitation to get away for the weekend for us to decide we need to relegate that big job of empathy for another day. If you are struggling with feeling like what you're giving is inadequate, know this: you are probably doing great.

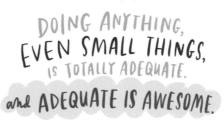

DOING ANYTHING, EVEN SMALL THINGS, IS TOTALLY ADEQUATE. and ADEQUATE IS AWESOME.

PART THREE:

JUST HELP ME
NOT BE A
DISASTER

CHAPTER 6:
Please NEVER SAY THIS
(THANKS!)

"My uncle fancied himself a spiritual mentor and said,
'I see this as a sign of unresolved issues between you and
your mother.' Fuck. You."

—Heather, a cancer survivor

KELSEY Says:

Carla is a good friend of mine, and a very optimistic person. When she started losing her vision, the doctors couldn't figure out why. Naturally enough, she was having a hard time getting through all the medical tests, and the results had started pointing in one terrifying direction.

Carla called me the day she learned the news: she had multiple sclerosis. This was worse than I had been expecting. But Carla, ever the optimist, said she was actually feeling pretty relieved to know and pretty hopeful overall. She said that the doctors told her it can take a long time for the symptoms to progress, and that so long as she didn't turn completely blind, she was, for the time being, feeling sort of okay about it.

I paused for a few seconds, not wanting to feed my friend a load of optimistic horseshit. I also wanted her to know that I could handle the news, no matter how bad it got, and that I didn't need it to be sugarcoated. But how could I validate the gravity of Carla's situation while showing her that I was a good friend and could handle really bad news?

I told Carla the story of a college friend who had MS. Her condition got so bad that she ended her life by starving herself to death.

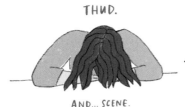

THUD.

AND... SCENE.

PS: Thanks to Carla's gracious understanding and forgiveness, our friendship remains incredibly close, and I went on to learn a bunch of better ways to support a friend.

In his memoir *A Grief Observed*, C. S. Lewis writes about the loss of his wife to cancer: "I see people as they approach me, trying to make up their minds whether they'll say something about it or not. I hate if they do, and if they don't." We are mercurial creatures in times of loss and transition, so the reality is there is no silver bullet when it comes to being there for someone in her darkest hour. It's important, however, to not make things worse.

OUR DEFENSES
CAN BE OFFENSIVE.

A lot of our screwups, in our attempts to be comforting, are the result of subliminal impulses that psychologists—and most laypeople—refer to as "defense mechanisms." These are the ways that our mind protects us from psychological pain. Often, they are helpful features of our psyche, but sometimes, our efforts to shield us from pain can get in the way of our being supportive. We'll describe a few of these defenses, and then you can see how they play out in some common "yikes, don't say this" scenarios.

·DENIAL This is when we don't accept reality or the facts because they're too painful. We simply pretend that the bad thing is not happening.

·PROJECTION This is when we attribute our own thoughts and feelings to someone else who does not have those thoughts and feelings.

·DISPLACEMENT This is when a person's new trauma brings up our old trauma from the past. It can even make us get more emotional now than when we first experienced the hardship. (One example would be getting really angry at your friend's recent ex because you never got to express that anger at your own ex.)

·INTELLECTUALIZATION When we want to avoid feeling emotional pain, our intellect can take over. Instead of feeling for someone, we analyze them or their situation.

When you read a lot of the "don't say this" examples in this chapter, you can rest assured that these impulses are completely natural. And yet, as natural as they may be, they should be restrained.

ME! ME! ME! PS: ME.

You know how it goes: You're telling a story about an incredibly hard thing in your life, like the time you had back surgery and couldn't walk for days. Your friend leans forward, and you think he's going to say something supportive. Instead, he says:

OMG I KNOW. THAT'S EXACTLY LIKE WHEN I SPRAINED MY THUMB IN THE DRESSING ROOM AT SAKS! I COULDN'T EVEN TEXT FOR A WEEK. AND THE PAIN!

Or you could be describing the heartbreak of yet *another* failed infertility treatment, and your friend pipes up with: "You guys should just go on vacation and relax. Worked great for me!" At the heart of many mistakes we make when trying to support someone is what we call "All About Me Syndrome." According to our research (and our own personal experience), AAMS happens a lot.

It makes sense, and we've all done it. Grasping for the right words, we try to relate, or pontificate, or do *something* to help us connect to the issue. If there's anything we feel comfortable talking about, it's our own lives, so when we're faced with someone else's unknown, uncomfortable scenario, it's natural to want to bring the conversation back to the familiar territory of our own personal experience.

COMPARISONS ARE ALWAYS ANNOYING.

When we're trying to relate to someone in their difficult time, our most common instinct is to compare it to our own situation. Like we describe on page 120 in chapter 4, when doing so, it may seem altruistic to help someone not feel alone. But in fact, comments such as "I know how you feel" or "That's so much like what happened to me" can close off opportunities to learn what the person in crisis is feeling. As one divorced person said: "My mother believed that my divorce would be just like hers. She didn't want to, or couldn't, see that my divorce was different, that *I* am different!" As someone who lost both parents said: "In general, I'm surprised by how folks are quick to start telling their own story but not really care about yours."

That doesn't mean you can't say that something similar happened to you, but if you do, be very mindful to say little more than that, and keep the conversation focused on the other person.

Theresa learns that her colleague, Richard, just lost his mother.

THERESA

I'm sorry about your mother.

RICHARD

Thank you. She struggled with cancer for two years. It finally got the best of her.

THERESA

My father died of a sudden heart attack five years ago. We didn't even have a chance to say good-bye.

RICHARD

Wow, Theresa, I'm sorry to hear that.

THERESA

You must feel relieved you could at least be there when she died.

In response to Theresa's comments about feeling relieved, Richard has a few unappealing options if he wants to continue the conversation:

1. "Yeah, I guess I am relieved."

2. "Not really relieved, no. It was terrible to watch her waste away in so much pain."

3. "Perhaps I should feel grateful I was with her at the end."

BREAKDOWN: Theresa's conversational tactics include two common pitfalls. First, by comparing her experience to Richard's, she changes the point of the conversation, which was empathy for Richard, to empathy for her, thus obligating Richard to address *her* feelings. Second, she is assuming, based on her own experience of disappointment at not being present when her father died, that Richard *should* experience relief at being present when his mother died.

Richard's first response is to agree he is relieved, but with ambivalence, and so he doesn't get to authentically express how he feels. Richard's second response is *very* authentic, but defensive, meaning the conversation no longer feels supportive. Richard's third response suggests he is avoiding Theresa's judgment and unconvincingly acquiesces to "feeling grateful." But mostly he's probably just feeling annoyed by Theresa.

Let's try this again:

THERESA

I hear you just lost your mother.

RICHARD

Thank you. She struggled with cancer for two years. It finally got the best of her.

To offer better support, Theresa has a few alternative responses:

1. "I'm so sorry." [Here, she ignores her own experience.]

2. "I'm sorry to hear that. I lost my father a few years ago. How are you doing?" [Here, she acknowledges going through something similar but keeps the focus on Richard's feelings.]

3. "How was it seeing her go at the end of her life?" [Here, if Theresa wants to avail herself to hear more about Richard's experience at the end of his mother's life, she can ask about it. In so doing, she uses her own experience to infer its importance, but not to assume Richard's feelings.]

This one's important, so let's see another example.

Take a look at a conversation that happened with one of our interviewees, Kelly, when she told her friend Jen over the phone about her recent diagnosis of cancer:

KELLY

I have breast cancer.

JEN

Wow. Well, at least they know a lot about your kind. Because, you know I have cancer too. And they don't know anything about my kind of cancer.

KELLY

Yeah, I guess it's good. Right. Um . . . except this kind of breast cancer is unique. Only 15 percent of breast cancers are "triple negative," and they don't have a lot of research on how to treat it other than with intense chemotherapy.

JEN

Well, I have to take a chemo pill every day to handle my cancer. And the effects are awful.

Well, um. My cancer is so aggressive, they're giving me the maximum dose, which will be awful for like six months. Is your chemo pill the maximum dose?

No, but it still makes me tired. And I will have to take it for life. Yours will be over in six months.

(approaching tears) Right, but at least you know that by taking your chemo pill you'll survive. Right? I don't know that!

You'll probably survive.

(click)

Now, this is an extreme case of AAMS. However, it really did happen. And we can see how it could: Kelly's friend was stressed about her own situation. Rightly so! However, maybe Jen wasn't quite ready to speak to Kelly yet about her cancer diagnosis, because it was bringing up feelings about her own health. She couldn't get out of her own problems long enough to be supportive in that conversation. This phenomenon is something that support groups are well aware of, and it's why a common ground rule is about no one person's situation being any worse or better than another's. If you show up at a support group because you're scared or feeling alone, then it doesn't matter if you're stage 1 or stage 3, because what matters is that you feel, well, scared and alone. As one woman we interviewed said, on people with healthy children who compare them to her child, who has special health needs: "No matter the intention, comparisons just don't help." End of story.

YOU'RE NOT AN EXPERT

As it turns out, if you've got the Internet, you can be an expert and create a theory on anything. Wine causes cancer. Miscarriages can be a result of too much coffee—or not enough coffee. Getting a divorce? There was an article just this past Sunday about how everyone else is too. That's right, your marriage crumbling is just a generational thing! You're not special; we'll send you the link.

When it comes to being supportive, being smart matters way less than being kind (and well mannered). It's fine if you have a theory about why your uncle has lung cancer, but he doesn't need to hear your opinions *now*. As one woman explained to Kelsey regarding her mother's oral cancer diagnosis:

> *"It was annoying that everyone asked if she was a smoker. Yes, she had smoked when she was younger, in the 1970s. But does that mean she deserved to get cancer? The question implied she 'asked for it,' and it felt totally unsympathetic."*

UNLESS YOU ACTUALLY ARE an EXPERT, WHOSE EXPERTISE IS BEING ASKED FOR, HEARING NEWS OF SOMEONE'S CRISIS IS NOT THE TIME to OFFER UP CASUAL THEORIES ABOUT THEIR MISFORTUNE.

Doing this leads to two hurtful implications: (1) the event was preventable and/or deserved, because if this person had only done X or Y instead they would be fine, and (2) your fact-finding mission is less about providing comfort than about "weeding out" the source of a problem—to make sure it doesn't happen to you. A woman Kelsey interviewed was diagnosed with cancer and said about people asking her questions: "It feels like people are trying to use my situation to calculate their own risks."

When you want to reach out to a person going through something that you've also experienced yourself, you can now see why it's a good idea to restrain your normal, but incredibly unhelpful impulse to compare your situations. If you don't feel prepared to handle someone else's difficulty because of the intense feelings it brings up about your own, take a look at the Empathy Menu on page 155 and explore other ways of being there for your friend that don't involve much talking about it. And if you want to talk about the feelings that are coming up for you as a result of a friend's difficult time, talk to others about what's going on—not your suffering friend.

PLEASE STOP WITH THE WORST-CASE SCENARIOS.

YOU'RE HAVING A KID? I HOPE YOU'RE SLEEPING NOW! BECAUSE YOU KNOW YOU WON'T SLEEP FOR YEARS ONCE THE BABY COMES! SERIOUSLY, YEARS!

Whether it's a comment on how much sleep deprivation a new parent should expect, or a listing of the statistics surrounding death rates and lung cancer, people do not feel comforted by worst-case scenarios. Even if they're a pessimist, hearing someone else echo their worst fears is pretty much the opposite of comforting. Kelsey was surprised by her reaction to worst-case-scenario stories, as she's generally someone most likely to see the glass half empty with a microbe of some infectious disease in the water. But when people would commonly mention a relative or friend who died of breast cancer, she found herself nearly heading to the toilet to throw up because she was so freaked out.

IT'S SAFE to ASSUME THAT THEY'VE GOOGLED THEIR OWN SITUATION A LOT MORE THAN SOMEONE WHO ISN'T LIVING IT EVERY DAY.

What's more, by offering up a worst-case scenario, you're not sharing any information with the suffering person that they probably don't already know. Someone who is about to be a new parent already knows their sleep is about to be permanently disrupted—got it, thanks!—and a person with lung cancer is probably all too aware of their own mortality. We get that your friend doesn't want to hear a bunch of optimistic BS, but your friend doesn't want to hear this incredibly depressing and scary version of the future, either. Who would? As much as this rule requires considerable restraint for some, it's best to remember:

WORST-CASE SCENARIOS MAKE PEOPLE FEEL EVEN MORE AFRAID THAN THEY ALREADY DID.

WHen LIFE GIVES you LEMONS, I WON'T TELL you A STORY ABOUT MY Cousin's FRIEND WHO DIED oF LEMONS.

Juan learns that his sister, Sue, is getting divorced.

*Juan, I have some hard news to share.
Carlos and I are getting divorced.*

*What? Oh, wow. That's insane! How did
this happen?*

Well, it's been coming for a while.

But you always seemed so happy!

There's a lot to it.

*But what about the house and kids?
How the hell are you going to get by?*

SUE

You know, this kind of thing happens to people all the time. The kids won't even notice it happened. In fact, I am great! *[Sue then hangs up and sobs, doubts her entire existence, and wants to punch Juan.]*

BREAKDOWN: Juan's panicked reaction to Sue's news is rooted in concern, but his astonishment makes Sue feel judged, and his line of questioning makes her feel like he has zero faith in her ability to cope. Juan's doomsday panic makes Sue want to:

1. Avoid his judgment; and

2. Reassure him. She does this by normalizing what she is going through: "It happens all the time," and "It happens to lots of people." Sue ends up having to both defend herself and comfort Juan, which is the opposite of how Juan probably intended for this to go down.

Why did Juan do this? It may be he is truly concerned about Sue, knowing, for example, that she and her husband just took on a major loan to buy their house. Or he is bringing his own fears into the situation, because he has contemplated these things against getting a divorce himself. One woman Kelsey spoke to described her father's concern about her getting divorced. He asked that she try harder to save her marriage, but six months after she filed *her* divorce papers, her parents filed theirs. The point is: our own fears can come up when someone describes their difficult situation. Our job is to not act on those fears with a line of questioning or giving advice, but simply to find out how the person is doing.

Let's try this again:

SUE

Juan, I have some hard news.
Carlos and I are getting divorced.

JUAN

Wow! That is surprising. How are you doing?
[Here, Juan suggests surprise without panic.
He doesn't ask "What happened?," assuming
he will learn in time. He also shows interest
in Sue's feelings by immediately turning the
conversation back to how she is doing.]

Here's another option for Juan:

JUAN

There are lots of things you must be thinking
about right now. How are you doing? [Here,
Juan is showing his concern by validating
the hurdles that lie ahead of Sue without
suggesting she is ignorant of them, and he
makes it clear that he's available to talk
more about her feelings.]

BuT WAIT!
UNBRIDLED OPTIMISM
MIGHT BE WORSE.

It can be hard for the optimistically inclined among us to hear, but optimistic reactions, ones that people who are grieving might consider *irrationally* optimistic, can be even tougher to bear than pessimistic reactions. For people in crisis, ill-timed optimism just feels like a meaningless empty platitude, especially for a situation that *really might not get better*.

Research backs this up: unbridled positivity in an experience of failure or distress makes people feel worse, not better. What ours and the experience of many others also confirms is that putting a positive spin on something difficult usually winds up feeling like an effort to get the griever to stop talking about it, making the griever shut down (and stop calling you).

YOU MAY VERY WELL BELIEVE THAT EVERYTHING HAPPENS FOR A REASON, OR THAT GOD HAS a PLAN. MANY PEOPLE DO. BUT THESE ARE YOUR BELIEFS, and UNLESS YOU KNOW THAT THE SUFFERING PERSON SHARES THEM, THEY LIKELY WON'T SERVE AS COMFORT THE WAY THEY MIGHT FOR YOU.

Eventually, with time and perspective, the person in crisis may be able to look back on this time in their lives and think, *You know what, I can see how X good thing came out of that terrible event*. Making meaning out of horrible situations does help people cope with them. But that kind of benefit is something we each arrive at (or not) on our own, in our own time. No amount of force-fed positivity will help, unless the suffering person is ready to go there. And in the immediate aftermath of a diagnosis, death, or loss, very few people are.

YOUR JOB IS to HEAR, NOT REDUCE SOMEONE'S WORRY.

UNHELPFUL STATEMENTS

- "EVERYTHING HAPPENS FOR A REASON."

- "THIS IS GOD'S PLAN."

- "WHAT DOESN'T KILL YOU MAKES YOU STRONGER."

- "IT COULD BE WORSE."

- "AT LEAST IT'S NOT CANCER."

- "JUST THINK POSITIVE THOUGHTS."

- "GOD DOESN'T GIVE YOU MORE THAN YOU CAN HANDLE."

- "AT LEAST YOU HAVE ONE HEALTHY CHILD."

- "YOU CAN ALWAYS JUST ADOPT."

- REALLY, ANYTHING BEGINNING WITH "JUST" OR "AT LEAST."

EMPATHY TIP: If fix-it platitudes are so unhelpful, why are they so common? Val Walker, in her book, *The Art of Comforting*, argues that our culture values production over presence, and organization over emotional mess. We believe in getting things done rather than just letting things be, and we believe that "healing" means *getting over* rather than *learning to live with* the loss. Our discomfort with suffering, and our rush to make it stop, can result in simpleminded fixes that suggest the problem of grief is an easy one to get over. This superficial effort just makes the suffering person feel even more broken (and pathetic) for suffering at all, and more detached from the person trying to help.

For all these reasons, it's best to avoid look-on-the-bright-side phrases and platitudes. Instead, find out how your friend is feeling about what's going on.

It's simple: just listen.

PLEASE LET ME BE THE FIRST TO PUNCH THE NEXT PERSON WHO TELLS YOU EVERYTHING HAPPENS FOR A REASON.

I'M SORRY YOU'RE GOING THROUGH THIS.

Here, Mardie is telling her neighbor Wendy about her child's diagnosis:

I can't sleep. I'm a wreck. She is getting a psychological workup. The doctors say based on her history and what they've seen so far, it's more than fifty percent likely that she has Tourette's syndrome.

Don't worry. They didn't say a one hundred percent chance.

Instead of hearing Mardie's worry, in this dialogue Wendy tries to reduce it with a positive view of the odds.

I don't know, more than a fifty percent chance isn't a one percent chance. There's a fifty percent chance I'll have a cheeseburger tonight, meaning I really might. So my kid really might have a disorder. You know?

Everything will be okay. You have to stay positive.

Here, Wendy inserts her own belief system about what causes good health outcomes. By doing this, she implies:

1. Mardie's belief system is inadequate and is the cause of her suffering.

2. Mardie's failure to stay "positive enough" may even be the root cause of her child's condition, and this failing somehow means Mardie willed it to happen, or the family deserved it. Let's try this again:

I can't sleep. I'm a wreck. The doctors say based on what they've seen so far, it's more than fifty percent likely that she has Tourette's.

I am so sorry this is happening.

Thank you. I don't know what to do. I guess all I can do is wait and see. And stay off the Internet. But it's so hard.

Wendy's simple acknowledgment of this difficult news opens up a lot of trust for Mardie to then talk more about how she's feeling.

EMPATHY TIP: Follow their lead. If you ask the person in crisis how they're feeling, and *they* respond with unbridled optimism or a phrase that you would consider to be a platitude, it's okay to follow their lead and mirror their language. Your positive perspective, in this case, would likely be helpful.

RESIST
ARMCHAIR QUARTERBACKING

It's hard to resist sharing the twenty-twenty hindsight that comes to us so clearly in the time of someone else's difficulty (but so rarely in times of our own). But it's *never ever* the right thing to do.

INSTEAD OF THIS	TRY THIS
"I never did like him." *"I thought you would hate that job."* *"I knew you shouldn't have moved near that landfill."* *"I could see the signs."* *"I'm surprised you didn't do this sooner."* *"You have to pay to play."*	*Zip it!*

FIREFIGHTERS ARE HEROES
(NOT ME)

EMILY Says:

When I was having chemo, I heard "Oh, you're so brave!" a lot. I appreciated that people were just trying to be complimentary, but it also made me feel like nobody had any idea what having cancer was like. People who choose to run into burning buildings to save strangers are brave. I was just stuck in a shitty situation that I would have given anything to get out of, and the only way to do that was to just keep waking up every day and putting one foot in front of the other.

It's not crazy to want to encourage and embolden your friend. We've all had feelings of defeat and insecurity, so we know how important it can be in those times for loved ones to cheer us on with how awesome and special we are.

Sometimes, too, our difficult times are a long and exhausting road. Living with a chronic illness is a good example of this. When this is our reality, we need to feel seen for the tenacity it takes just to get up in the morning, instead of judged for any complaints we might have. (And hard times can make all of us complain. A lot.)

However, unless you know a lot about someone's particular situation, it's best to skip making observations and affirmations about how they're handling it. When these comments come from people who don't know all the ins and outs of a situation, a well-intentioned phrase like "You are so brave" can sometimes sound like "Your life is so awful I can't imagine living it." And that kind of admiration, for the act of waking up and doing what you need to do to get through the day, can feel less like genuine awe, and more like the pity we discuss on page 64.

Another possible, undesirable side effect of a comment like "You are so strong" is that it puts the suffering person on a pedestal and can make them feel reluctant to be "real" with their emotions, for fear of letting others down or burdening them by sharing the real pain they may be going through. As Kelsey was told by a woman after she lost her spouse: "I cringed when people said 'You are so strong.' I may have appeared strong, but I was falling apart inside. I was surviving only because of Paxil."

SCENARIO 1:
Mindy has a six-year-old daughter who has cerebral palsy and uses a wheelchair. She is helping her daughter navigate the chair through a tight bathroom doorway at the movie theater. She runs into Priya, the mother of her daughter's classmate, who is standing in line. They chitchat idly for about ten seconds about the movie. And then, after a pause:

You know, Mindy, I simply just don't know how you do it.

PRIYA

"Do what?" [She asks with dread.]

MINDY

Oh, you know, raise Samantha like that. Managing all the challenges. I just could never do it. You're amazing.

PRIYA

Given what you have read so far, you can take a guess at which of the following (likely unspoken) reactions Mindy has to Priya's comment:

1. Appreciation for Priya's support.

2. Annoyance at Priya's condescending pity.

You get a gold star if you picked number 2. Whether you got this answer right or wrong, consider why Mindy would feel annoyed rather than supported by this comment. Then imagine why, in this situation, the most compassionate way for Priya to be with Mindy would probably be to say nothing about her daughter's condition. To help, think about these questions:

1. What message is Mindy hearing from Priya's comment?

2. Why does Priya feel the need to make this comment? [The reasons could be both benevolent and condescending.]

3. What benefit would Mindy feel from not hearing a comment about her daughter's condition?

4. If Priya wants to connect with Mindy, what kind of observation, comment, or question about Mindy's daughter could Priya make that would help "normalize" her role as a mother, in the same way that Priya is also a mother?

SCENARIO 2: Joe has lived with multiple sclerosis for over fifteen years. His condition flares every now and then, and lately, his neuropathic pain has gotten worse. His fatigue is getting really bad, and he hasn't been able to go to work for the last five days. It causes him pain to do it, but he still walks his dog every day and is reading to his children before they go to bed. His younger brother, John, has been staying with the family for a few months as John tries to get his life together.

JOHN

Joe, seeing you do what you do with the pain and fatigue you have . . . it has been making me think. My anger issues and hotheadedness cause me a lot of problems at work and with my marriage. Seeing you handle this, just doing what you have to do, I am learning so much by your example. I know you never signed up for this disease or for being my hero. But right now, seeing you with your kids and that goofball of a poodle, I give you major respect.

JOE

You sound like a goofball yourself, man. But seriously, thanks. I needed that. Especially now. I feel so lame that I haven't been able to get to the office this week.

JOHN

That's a bummer. From where I sit, though, you are doing an incredible job. What's going on?

We all need to be picked up when we are feeling down, and hearing that we are doing a really great job or that we're amazing (because we really are) when we are feeling quite the opposite is a godsend. If you don't know the nature of someone's particular struggle, however, it's ultimately best to avoid specific statements about how that person is managing it.

IF THEY DIDN'T ASK YOU, THEY PROBABLY DON'T WANT to KNOW.

We all know unsolicited advice can be annoying, even if it's useful. Yet, when something is wrong, many of us instinctively move toward trying to solve the problem. That's when we I-wanna-be-helpful types start rattling off the benefits of headstands for fertility.

As tempting as it can be to offer up your gem of knowledge that will fix someone else's problem, 99 percent of the time, *your friend doesn't want to hear your advice.* But don't take it personally. You can rest assured that you are not the only one with *really good* advice to give.

PEOPLE in THEIR DARKEST HOUR HEAR ENOUGH ADVICE to MAKE a PERSON CRAZY.

And as the advice starts piling up, it gets even crazier to manage, because it inevitably gets contradictory. Macrobiotic diets versus raw. Plant-based versus Paleo. Native American versus Chinese herbal extracts. Mediators versus attorneys. IVF versus adoption. And on (and on) it goes.

Meanwhile, one can rest assured that the person who is living with a difficulty is thinking about how to approach their situation twenty-four hours a day, seven days a week, and they've probably put way more time than you have into figuring out what to do. As a mother described about her daughter's unusual health condition, one that took years to diagnose:

> *"For years, people told me what to feed her and what doctors I should visit, when I had already explored those options. What did they think, that I hadn't looked into it? It is my* child *that is sick."*

ADVICE *is* MADDENING, BUT ITS MOST SIGNIFICANT FLAW *is* HOW JUDGMENTAL IT CAN FEEL *to* HEAR IT. As one woman struggling with fertility told Kelsey, advice about her infertility made her problem feel "merit based," as if only women doing daily yoga while drinking kombucha deserved to get pregnant. By the same logic, those that don't take the "helper's" advice deserve to struggle. Fearing this kind of judgment is highly rational, because research shows what we instinctively know: that we feel less compassion toward people when we believe they're the cause of their own problems. To learn more about our tendencies to give advice, read about Foisters on page 76.

SO WHAT to DO WHEN FACED WITH the LURE OF ADVICE-GIVING?

1. **AVOID SUGGESTING CURES.** Though the instinct may come from the right place, remember: force-feeding your sick friend wheatgrass, or some other thing you read about online, is not helpful.

2. **AVOID THE WORD "SHOULD."** If you have entered a house of sorrow, and you feel the word *should* crossing your lips, *stop talking*. There's probably food around—eat something instead.

3. **AVOID ALL OF THESE:**

WHY NOT ADOPT INSTEAD OF DOING IVF?

HAVE YOU TRIED YOGA?

WHAT ABOUT COUPLES COUNSELING?

I READ THAT MEAT CAUSES CANCER.

HAVE YOU LOOKED FOR A JOB ON CRAIGSLIST?

I'VE HEARD EATING RAW FOODS WILL CURE YOU.

What to say instead? Going back to our recommendations on what to say on page 131, try "I trust that you know what to do." *If you must,* because you have some kind of deep, specialized knowledge and experience regarding the person's situation, and you'd feel like a terrible person if you didn't offer advice, you can add to that statement something like "If you want any extra info on XYZ, I can give that to you." If you do offer information, however, you are strongly advised to end that overture with "But I imagine you've got it covered."

YOU GET IT, RIGHT? IT'S NOT YOUR JOB to MAKE SUGGESTIONS RIGHT NOW. REMEMBER, SUFFERING PEOPLE ARE IN CHARGE OF THEIR OWN EXPERIENCES. UNLESS THEY ASK FOR YOUR SUGGESTION OR FEEDBACK, ASSUME THEY KNOW EVERYTHING THERE IS to KNOW, and THAT THEY'VE CHOSEN to HANDLE THINGS THEIR WAY FOR a VERY GOOD REASON.

A great rule of thumb when supporting someone in a hard time echoes the Hippocratic oath in medicine: "Do no harm." Resist the problem-solving urge; resist the urge to be smart and "fix" it. Take comfort in the fact that life gives us plenty of other opportunities to prove how smart we are.

What to do instead?

EMBRACE THE AWKWARD SILENCE.
YOU'LL LIVE THROUGH IT JUST FINE.

MY FRIEND IS DRIVING ME INSANE AND I CAN'T DEAL
(BUT I FEEL SO GUILTY EVEN THINKING THAT BECAUSE HER LIFE IS SO HARD RIGHT NOW)
HELP!

Sometimes, hard times can leave a suffering person so stuck in their sadness or anger or fear that they keep repeating the same harmful behaviors over and over. This type of pattern may make it *very hard* for the person's friends and family to stay quiet and listen without trying to "fix it." Sometimes, our complaints or frustration with the person are momentary, and it's okay to share those feelings with others (but not with the person at the center of the problem). Other times, however, they are causing a real rift in the relationship.

When a loved one's personal trial is so consuming that there's no room for you in the relationship anymore, it's easy to get frustrated, and it's natural to get to a point where you just want to set them straight and get back to "normal."

The best way to approach this challenge is to focus on where your heart is. Leave aside the advice you'd love to give, and simply talk to the person about how you're feeling about the relationship the two of you now have.

SAYING HOW YOU ARE FEELING is a LOT HARDER THAN TELLING SOMEBODY WHAT TO DO, BUT IT'S a FAR MORE VULNERABLE, and TRUSTWORTHY, PLACE to BEGIN.

Here's a chart laying out common impulses and our recommended actions.

INSTEAD OF THIS	TRY THIS
Giving advice	*Don't advise; exercise restraint.*
Being tired of listening to it	*Don't advise; be patient.*
Ending the relationship over it	*Talk about what's hardest to say: how you are feeling about your relationship in light of this hard time.*

This is all so much tougher than giving advice, but when you really listen to your friend, you'll hear something far more rewarding than the empty echo of your own brilliance.

We know this is going to feel superhard. It will get easier over time. If you take nothing else away from this section, remember this:

ALMOST NEVER, EVER DOLE OUT ADVICE at ALL.

TRY NOT to BE THAT ANNOYING PERSON

INSTEAD OF THIS	TRY THIS
"You must feel ____."	*"I'm sorry."*
"I know how you feel."	*"Wow, that can be hard."*
"I felt ____ when I ____."	*"What's that like for you?"*
"What happened to me was ____."	*"That happened to me, but I want to know: How are you?"*
"You should try ____."	*Advise nothing, or only offer a resource if it's requested.*
"Did this happen because you ____?"	*"What is known about why this happened?" (Ask "why" questions cautiously.)*
"Oh no! But what about ____?"	*Be concerned, but stay calm and proffer no examples of worst-case scenarios.*
"I wouldn't worry."	*Listen to the source of worry.*
"You're a saint! / I could never do it . . ."	*"You're doing a great job under the circumstances."*

THE BOTTOM LINE:
EMPATHY is NOT
TELLING SOMEONE HOW to FEEL.

SQUELCH THE FOLLOWING IMPULSES:

- SUGGESTING THAT YOU KNOW HOW SOMEONE FEELS
- IDENTIFYING THE CAUSE OF THE PROBLEM
- TELLING SOMEONE WHAT THEY SHOULD DO ABOUT THEIR HARD TIME
- REACTING WITH PESSIMISM
- MINIMIZING PEOPLE'S CONCERNS
- BRINGING "PERSPECTIVE" to a SITUATION WITH FORCED POSITIVITY OR PLATITUDES
- TELLING SOMEONE HOW STRONG OR SAINTLY THEY ARE

Too often, efforts at comforting a suffering person are made before that person is asked how they're feeling. We want to help by fixing, but that often implies the "fixer" is right, and the person being fixed is "defective" for not having "solved" the problem on their own. When such attempts to comfort don't work, it's not a problem of the sufferer being unappreciative—it's simply that the consoler failed to connect.

Instead:

ASK. LISTEN. LEARN.

For a griever, there is rarely any more comfort than companionship on the awful path of sorrow. Hopefully, that path will also include joy in time. But there is no guarantee that it will, and there is no timeline for when it does. There is no human gain in shying away from that reality, as difficult as it may feel. That is the plight of the griever; that is the plight of the witness.

CHAPTER 7: EMPATHY DIRECTORY: DOs and DON'Ts CHEAT SHEETS

If you're looking for some quick information to help someone in an immediate crisis, you're in the right place. Even if you've memorized every exercise and topic covered in this book, this directory is a handy reference of dos and don'ts for hard times such as loss, illness, divorce, and other situations that inevitably come our way.

We all know you can't "cheat-sheet" your way into meaningful connections. (Why can't life just be organized into bullet points?) But the tables and tips on the coming pages can definitely help you feel more confident in offering support, and help those in crisis feel more supported.

AT a GLANCE: ILLNESS / CHRONIC HEALTH PROBLEM

INTENT	INSTEAD OF THIS	TRY THIS
EMPATHY	"I can't believe this is happening to you." "But isn't this fatal?" "But your house isn't handicap accessible!" "Oh, how awful . . ." "But you don't look sick." "But you're so young . . ."	"I am sorry you are going through this." "This sucks." (You may be corrected that it doesn't; or it may be just the right thing to hear. When in doubt, ask.) "I want you to know I am here for you if there is anything I can do." "I can help you with ____ and I am free most Tuesdays if that works." "You don't look sick; how are you actually doing?" "I understand you had to break plans. No worries—let's try again." "Before I finalize the reservation, I'll just confirm they are wheelchair accessible." (Or not mention you are checking and just check.)
RELATE	"I had (my brother had) ____ and I know how it feels." "You know, we all feel ____ from time to time. Don't worry." "That happened to my sister, and it wasn't that big of a deal." "We all feel a little tired at the end of the day."	"I can't imagine what you are going through. What's that like for you?" "How are you feeling, today?" "I am sorry."

INTENT	INSTEAD OF THIS	TRY THIS
PERSPECTIVE	*"Any of us could get hit by a bus."* *"At least it's not ____ (kind of illness)."* *"At least it's treatable."* *"It's only 30 percent odds . . ."* *"They call that the good cancer, though, right?"* *"You are so lucky to not have to work. Think about it like a permanent vacation."*	*"I know someone with this diagnosis and she is doing totally great now. I don't know if this will be the case for you, but I hope so."* *"What's it like for you, today?"* *"How do you feel about not being able to work in a paid job?"*
INTEREST	*"Do they know why you got this?"* *"Did you ever smoke?"*	*"Is there anything the doctors can say about it now?"* *"How are you feeling about what happened?"* *"What's it like to ____ ?"*
HOPE/ RESOLVE	*"You can get through this. My cousin did."* *"You are so strong. You are a fighter."* *"You are so brave."* *"You just have to get out of the house!" (Or whatever change in lifestyle you think a sick person has to make.)*	*"I have seen you manage really tough things in the past and I know you can get through this."* *"You don't have to be strong for me."* *"Tell me how I can support you the most."* *"How about we try ____ (basically anything that nudges someone out of their malaise-filled comfort zone), and if it's uncomfortable, we'll stop immediately."*

A FEW THOUGHTFUL GESTURES:

♥ Got me a pair of socks that said
   "I'm so high, I don't care."

♥ Brought me a stuffed animal, which even a sarcastic
   adult like myself appreciated.

♥ Gave us a jar of quarters to pay for parking/bought us
   parking passes.

♥ Our son was in a coma, and friends shared the load
   and visited him in the hospital.

♥ Made me several playlists with different themes for
   different moods.

♥ Friends of a friend whom I barely knew came by
   the rehabilitation center with their guitars
   and sang me songs.

♥ Sent me a deep-dish pizza from a
   restaurant in my hometown of Chicago.

♥ Made me a book of redeemable "friend coupons."

♥ Paid for someone to come over and clean my house while
   I was in the hospital.

♥ Hung inexpensive prints from my favorite artists all over my hospital room.

♥ Took my daughter to school three days a week so I could get to outpatient treatment.

AT a GLANCE: DIVORCE

INTENT	INSTEAD OF THIS	TRY THIS
EMPATHY	*"Have you thought about counseling?"* *"Are you sure you want to do this?"* *"She was a jerk anyway."*	*"How are you doing?"* *"How do you feel about your process in getting to this point?"* *"Wow, that can be hard."*
RELATE	*"Didn't ____ down the street get divorced?"* *"We've all been there."*	*"I went through ____ (kind of experience), and I had those same feelings."* *"My brother, who I greatly admire, went through a similar experience."*
PERSPECTIVE	*"You will find someone else."* *"I saw this coming—you two weren't meant for each other."* *"I had a feeling the relationship was unstable for a while."*	*The best time to try offering perspective is a few months (or more) after the separation:* *"Once this is all over, I truly believe you will be happier for this."*

INTENT	INSTEAD OF THIS	TRY THIS
INTEREST	*"How are the kids holding up?"* *"Have you started dating yet?"* *"What happened?"* *"Do you think he/she was cheating?"*	*"How did ____ (court case, moving, talk with the ex . . .) go?"* *Only if there is time for a real answer, then: "How are you feeling about ____ (finances, moving, kids, etc.)?"* *"Of course I am curious about what led to this, but I just hope that you are doing okay and we can talk about what happened whenever/if ever you want to."*
HOPE/ RESOLVE	*"You shouldn't let her push you around anymore."*	*"I trust you are doing the right thing/will know how to handle yourself."* *"You are attractive and charming and a great catch!"*

A FEW THOUGHTFUL GESTURES:

♥ A girlfriend who lives across the country sent me a really funny gag gift about what to do when you break up. It was a wheel of retribution and it made me laugh—always a good thing.

♥ A friend had had balloons brought into my apartment to welcome me to my new place.

♥ My good friend got me a book of essays about going through divorce.

♥ My best friend had flowers waiting on my desk
when I got back from divorce court, which,
by the way, is the worst part.

♥ Coming over with a ton of ice cream as the
typical breakup food was really sweet—
and added a sense of humor to it too.

AT a GLANCE: FERTILITY STRUGGLES and MISCARRIAGE

INTENT	INSTEAD OF THIS	TRY THIS
EMPATHY	*"Have you thought about ____ (adoption, diet change, acupuncture, yoga)?"* *"Try to relax, go on vacation, limit your work schedule."* *"Just do anything."* *"There are so many foster kids that need homes, though!"*	*"How are you doing?"* *"If there is anything I can do, let me know."* *"How do you feel about your process in getting to this point?"* *"I have some thoughts or treatment experiences if you ever want to hear them; though I understand if you don't."*
RELATE	*"I tried for six months before anything happened."* *"Sometimes it just takes time."*	*"I've never been through infertility, but if you ever want to talk about it, I am here."* *"My brother went through a similar experience—if you have any questions I can put you in touch."*

INTENT	INSTEAD OF THIS	TRY THIS
PERSPECTIVE	"Don't worry, it eventually happened for me." "Parenthood is not all that it's cracked up to be." "You should come to the holiday event this year; it will make you feel better." "This was nature's way of ending a bad pregnancy." "It'll happen when you're truly ready."	"Wow, that can be hard." "How are you doing?" "If it's too hard to come to my baby shower, I completely understand." "I am sorry about your loss."
INTEREST	"Are you pregnant yet?" "How much does it cost?" "Whose problem is it?" If person miscarried: "How did it happen? What did you do?"	"How did the medical appointment go?" (If you are in the know about appointments.) "How are you feeling about ____ (finances, upcoming holiday events, or baby shower, etc.)?" "Any difficult side effects of the medication?" Ask several weeks after a miscarriage or failed fertility treatment: "How are you feeling about ____?"
HOPE/ RESOLVE	"I just know you will get pregnant!" "It just wasn't meant to be." "It wasn't God's plan." "At least you know you can get pregnant" (if the person miscarried).	"No matter how you do it, I know you will make a great parent." "I am glad you're still trying." "My brother and his wife did this for three years and, on the third try, it finally worked. That's my hope for you." "How are you feeling about it?"

A FEW THOUGHTFUL GESTURES:

♥ A dear friend wanted me to attend her child's birthday party, but being around kids was too hard. She then asked if I could help out with just hanging up the party decorations, also offering that I could leave before others arrived.

♥ I was single trying to get pregnant. My friend who took me to my insemination appointment also treated me to lunch afterward to mark this momentous occasion.

♥ Friends wanted to plan a summer vacation with us, and with the nature of infertility appointments, we couldn't firm anything up until the last minute. Even though it meant having fewer vacation options, they were very understanding.

♥ When saying I didn't want to be asked about being pregnant, anxious and excited friends who really wanted to know respected my wishes.

♥ After my miscarriage, a neighbor left me a plant at my door.

AT a GLANCE: LOSS

INTENT	INSTEAD OF THIS	TRY THIS
EMPATHY	"I can't believe this happened!!" "But how will you continue to support the family?!" "Who is going to pay for all of the expenses?!" "You really should move on."	"I am sorry you are going through this." "I'd like to help with the kids if I can. I am free to babysit." "People grieve in their own time, in their own way."
RELATE	"I lost my mother and I was devastated."	"I can't imagine what you are going through." "This is really hard." "How are you feeling, now?"
PERSPECTIVE	"Loss is a part of life." "At least he lived a full life." "At least you could see her in the end."	Let the grieving person come up with their own perspective. Accept that they may not.
INTEREST	"What kind of inheritance might you get?" "Did he smoke? Drink?"	"What are your next steps, and is there anything I can do to help?" "What was she like?" "What was your child's name?"
HOPE/ RESOLVE	"It's been six months. You should be over this by now." "You will find somebody else."	"Grief happens in its own time." "You will feel better one day, but I am here for you now."

A FEW THOUGHTFUL GESTURES:

♥ We were so grief stricken at the loss of our daughter that some people from our church made all the arrangements at our house for our son's birthday party. We didn't have to lift a finger.

♥ My friend created a beautiful announcement about my mother's passing that we posted outside our house.

♥ When my son killed himself, a colleague from work gave me a poem about loss.

♥ Friends helped me organize and clean up my mother's things. She was a hoarder and this was a really big job.

♥ When my good friend died in a car accident, work colleagues took me out to lunch.

♥ I never asked for it, but after my wife died, my neighbor swept up the leaves that accumulated every few days for about a month without ever mentioning it.

AT a GLANCE: UNEMPLOYMENT

INTENT	INSTEAD OF THIS	TRY THIS
EMPATHY	"I hope that your finances can manage this." "Wow, I can't imagine what that feels like." "Is your spouse handling the news okay?"	"This happened to me. It sucks." (Because this kind of incident brings a lot of shame.) Shoot them a LinkedIn request or write a recommendation on their online profile. "I really liked the work you were able to do here. I will miss you." "I'm here to talk if you need to."
PERSPECTIVE	"I wish I could have some time off!" "At least you are on unemployment." "When one door closes, another one opens."	"I know now this feels horrible, but you are so talented. Something will come up." "Let's get your mind off things. Let me take you out to dinner." (Or just treat without mentioning it.)
INTEREST	Asking "How's the job search?" every single day. "Have you sent out more résumés?" "Why did they fire you?" Sending random job leads and asking if the person followed up.	"Send me your résumé—I'll see if anyone I know would be interested." Pass on relevant job leads with "Maybe you know someone who'd be interested."

A FEW THOUGHTFUL GESTURES:

♥ A friend made me cupcakes that said "I love you."

♥ A colleague called after she heard the news and said how saddened she was to hear it.

♥ A colleague continued to send me relevant job leads and made introductions when it seemed worthwhile.

♥ A good friend gave me consulting work to get me over a financial hump.

♥ I couldn't afford to keep my hairstyle. My neighbor is a hairdresser and would style my hair for free before I had an interview.

♥ Some colleagues from my old work sent me LinkedIn requests.

♥ Friends networked in their neighborhood and found me a retail job.

♥ A colleague offered to be my reference when I was afraid I wouldn't have a good one.

CONCLUSION

YOU GOT THIS!

I'M INADEQUATE	I'M AWESOME
"I DON'T KNOW HOW."	"MY KINDNESS is MY CREDENTIAL."
"I DON'T KNOW WHAT to SAY."	"LISTENING SPEAKS VOLUMES."
"I DON'T HAVE THE BANDWIDTH."	"SMALL GESTURES MAKE a BIG DIFFERENCE."

The fear that we'll mess it up, the fear of saying something wrong, and the fear that we don't have the bandwidth to really help: these are the three things that most often get in the way of our reaching out to others. What these concerns essentially boil down to, though, is a simple lack of trust in ourselves, in what we already know how to do, and that who we are is enough.

IF WE WANT *to* BE SOMEONE PEOPLE TRUST *and* REACH OUT TO,
WE NEED *to* TRUST OURSELVES. **THAT DOESN'T MEAN BEING PERFECT.**
IT SIMPLY MEANS BEING WHO WE ARE.

1. TRUST *your* CONCERN:
- YOUR KINDNESS *is* YOUR CREDENTIAL.
- IF YOU CARE, YOUR CARE BELONGS.

2. TRUST *your* VALUES:
- PUT YOUR OWN OXYGEN MASK *on* FIRST.
- DON'T JUDGE OR ASSUME.

3. TRUST *your* BEHAVIOR:
- LISTENING SPEAKS VOLUMES ABOUT CARE.
- SMALL MOVES MAKE *a* BIG DIFFERENCE.

We can all have an important place in the lives of those around us, and we can take up as little or as much room in those lives as we can handle, or as the situation calls for. Once we trust our capacities to give and to accept the limits of our giving, we can give more freely, and with more joy. To do that, we need to move beyond our usual stories about others failing us, and about us failing others. We need to move toward being kinder and more accepting of our and others' shortcomings and differences, and, ultimately, toward richer, broader expressions of being human.

SHOWING UP FOR ONE ANOTHER WITH AUTHENTICITY and VULNERABILITY - and STICKING TOGETHER THROUGH LIFE'S HARD TIMES - IS WHAT BONDS US THE DEEPEST to EACH OTHER.

When we learn to connect with people in this way, we foster intimate and lasting, ride-or-die relationships. Ultimately, the moments of sorrow and fear we sit through together will also give us our moments of greatest nourishment, as both givers and receivers. So yeah: learning to show up can be scary. But is the temporary fear and discomfort worth it?

MORE THAN ANYTHING.

REFERENCES

Books for Normal Human Beings Having a Serious Day on the Beach

Brown, Brené. *Daring Greatly: How the Courage to Be Vulnerable Transforms the Way We Live, Love, Parent, and Lead.* New York: Gotham Books, 2012. Shows how our deepest fears of imperfection and vulnerability are, in fact, our greatest source of authentic connection.

Ehrenreich, Barbara. *Bright-Sided: How the Relentless Promotion of Positive Thinking Has Undermined America.* New York: Metropolitan Books, 2009. A sharp critique of a culture of positivity that can make people ashamed for feeling horrible in horrible situations.

Lerner, H. G. *The Dance of Fear: Rising Above Anxiety, Fear, and Shame to Be Your Best and Bravest Self.* New York: Perennial Currents, 2005. A classic providing a much needed review on how our reliance on the opinions of others and the negative ones we have of ourselves sabotage our self-esteem.

Lewis, C. S. (2001). *A Grief Observed*. San Francisco: HarperSanFrancisco, 2001.
A heartbreaking rendering of grief by theologian C. S. Lewis, who lost his wife to cancer. The best in its class.

Solomon, Andrew. *Far from the Tree: Parents, Children and the Search for Identity*. New York: Scribner, 2012.
Solomon's book provides an eye-opening glimpse into humanity's fraught and sublime conditions, awaking deep compassion without any hint of prescription or sanctimony.

Strayed, Cheryl. *Tiny Beautiful Things: Advice on Love and Life from Dear Sugar*. New York: Vintage Books, 2012.
Hands down, the best of its kind: advice loaded with searing honesty about life's vulnerable, complicated times.

Walker, Val. *The Art of Comforting: What to Say and Do for People in Distress*. New York: Jeremy P. Tarcher/Penguin, 2010.
A truly insightful account into dynamics of comfort and the culture in which it takes place.

Books for the Scientifically and Philosophically Curious

Overviews of Compassion Research and Debates

Keltner, Dacher. *Born to Be Good: The Science of a Meaningful Life*. New York: W. W. Norton & Company, 2009.

Krznaric, Roman. *Empathy: Why It Matters, and How to Get It*. New York: Penguin Group, 2014.

Monroe, K. R. *The Heart of Altruism: Perceptions of a Common Humanity*. Princeton, NJ: Princeton University Press, 1996.

Seppälä, Emma. *The Happiness Track: How to Apply the Science of Happiness to Accelerate Your Success*. San Francisco: HarperOne, 2016.

Workplace Compassion

Dutton, J., and Worline, M. *Awakening Compassion at Work: The Quiet Power That Elevates People and Organizations.* Oakland, CA: Berrett-Koehler Publishers, 2017.

Grant, A. M. *Give and Take: A Revolutionary Approach to Success.* New York: Viking, 2013.

Medical Compassion

Halpern, Jodi. *From Detached Concern to Empathy: Humanizing Medical Practice.* Oxford: Oxford University Press, 2001.

Halpern, S. P. *The Etiquette of Illness: What to Say When You Can't Find the Words.* New York: Bloomsbury, 2004.

Websites

Useful Research, Relatable Content, and Empathy Merchandise

Advice to Sink in Slowly: www.advicetosinkinslowly.org

Brain Pickings: www.brainpickings.org

CompassionLab: www.compassionlab.com

Emily McDowell Studio: www.emilymcdowell.com

Flower: www.flowerapp.com

Greater Good Science Center: www.greatergood.berkeley.edu

Help Each Other Out: www.helpeachotherout.org

ABOUT the RESEARCH

This book is based on an exploration with many people about what works and doesn't when giving support in difficult times. Some hard times weren't addressed because there wasn't enough data to do so. Other issues require a thorny mix of professional and community support and could not be responsibly addressed without more nuance. Some life situations, like parenting and "coming out," have a wide range of experiences from good to hard that didn't fit well in the set of issues elaborated on. All that being said, using your powers of empathy, it is reasonable to argue that concepts described here can guide you through any number of life's rough neighborhoods.

Responses came from over nine hundred participants to an online survey of open-ended questions and from fifty interviews.

People were asked about the kinds of words and gestures they found helpful in difficult situations and what was hard to hear from people ranging from strangers and colleagues to friends and family. In addition, over 450 participants across several empathy workshops, talks, and events completed "gesture cards" with similar information about how people stepped up and what efforts fell flat.

The survey and interview data was read and reread, then coded, categorized, and organized into themes that were distilled into the essential ideas presented in the book. In some cases, there were other also intriguing hints of themes regarding religion, humor, and touch, but ultimately there was not enough data to substantiate any claims, and we did not present them in the book. Themes that are presented in the book were cross-checked and developed with six readers, while several of the book's recommendations were verified with participants in several Empathy Bootcamp workshops.

Leaving no stone unturned, concepts and themes that came up in the questionnaire and interview data were supported with a thorough review of peer-reviewed studies found in journals addressing topics like divorce, infertility, illness, and loss, while concepts on matters like advice-giving and listening were supported by articles in communication studies, with liberties taken to adapt and greatly distill these ideas to make our recommendations actionable.

The final form of verification around themes from the data came from Kelsey's and Emily's own personal experiences. We are humans, after all, and through our collaboration made sure we could confidently stand behind the concepts, premises, and recommendations presented here. People shared their experiences and wisdom with us to benefit others in their similar situations. We hope their hard-earned wisdom can achieve that, while circling back to the person whose benefit matters most: you.

Caveat About the Data

The nature of our exploration of these topics did not allow us to thoroughly examine how issues of race, ethnicity, and culture play out in the kinds of gestures that are offered and how those are experienced. Participants in the survey and interviews and workshops were geographically, religiously, ethnically, sexually, and by gender diverse, and nothing we heard suggested providing comfort differently because of their background. However, some scholarship in communication studies suggests that a different approach with a focus on cultural and gender analysis would be able to find such differences if they are there, and it would be useful if such an exploration were done.

ACKNOWLEDGMENTS

KELSEY Says:

We can't get through shitty times like illness and loss by doing it alone. We can't birth ideas alone, either. This book would not have been possible without the support of many, many people.

Colleagues and a multitude of friends distributed my online research questionnaire and interview requests far and wide. Thanks to them, I was entrusted with the pain and hard-earned wisdom of several hundred people to whom I am forever grateful. Helping to harness their stories in order to explain comfort across many difficult times were Mardie Oakes, Jennie Mollica, Ed Dorrington, Dr. Amy D'Andrade, Dr. Mariah Breeding, and Dr. Beth Roy. They provided constructive feedback on emerging themes in the research and found the work's soul that my keep-me-out-of-the-doghouse-with-what-not-to-say perspective did not initially grasp. My good friend Katie Crouch showed me how humor can make a heavy subject engaging, Emily Han championed the book's practical focus, and Rob McQuilken taught me to take the reader on a journey of personal change.

The course of that journey became clear in the development of the Empathy Bootcamp workshop that is the basis of much of this book. Colleagues like Dr. Monica Worline from the University of Michigan's Compassion Lab and the brilliant therapist Kim Wylder helped me with insights into the corroding effect of shame on trusting our authentic capacity to give. Dr. Adam McTighe helped set the workshop's tone between research and relatability without cloying sentimentality, and the soulful young cancer survivor Meaghan Calcari Campbell wrote the poem that inspired the book's Empathy Menu. None of this would have been implemented, however, without Naomi Hoffer of the Helen Diller Cancer Center at the University of California, San Francisco, who brought in and championed this work, first launching it into the big wide world.

Many elements of the book are informed by activities supported by an organization I founded with several people called Help Each Other Out, which is trying to mainstream our society's capacity to deal with the human condition. More than two hundred people volunteered their time and donations to make the workshops, our public campaigns on Being There in several urban neighborhoods, and resource-rich website happen, providing the platform to write this book. Our advisory board has been responsible for fund-raising, networking, and thought partnership around every programmatic detail for three years, and they include Dr. Amy D'Andrade, Dr. Jan Malvin, Dr. Jen Tosti-Kharas, Liza Siegler, Michele Turner, Millicent Bogert, Mindy Schweitzer-Rawls, with additional loving help from Hope Singsen, the quiet powers of Maria Niubo, and constant support from Alex Armenta. The indefatigable Dara Kosberg lends her singular powers and passion as staff to officially move Help Each Other Out into its next developmental phase, and board member Mardie Oakes has been a supporter in nearly every part of the work, showing up always.

I am very fortunate to have several good friends that cared for this mission nearly as much as I did. My friend Amy D'Andrade may have cared even more. Since the beginning, she has dedicated her energies to develop every aspect of this work. From the research to the initial reading to the implementation of the workshops to the development of Help Each Other Out, she has been a thought partner and overall work-wife. All the while, she has been my very true friend. Thank you.

Good friends I have known since Earlham College patiently, enthusiastically, and supportively over the years asked, significantly helped, and asked again about how everything was going. Michele Belliveau, Deirdre Russo, Theresa Locklear, Lisa Long, Amy Hunter, Jessica Jones, and newer friends like my writing sister Calla Devlin, and my loving in-laws Dick and Sue Brown. All are like family to me, and I love them.

It was a big leap to craft the book we have now, and our editor Luke Dempsey at HarperOne took the plunge. He gave the manuscript a tough treatment when it needed it most; asking probing questions, being patient with revisions, and giving the faith I needed for us to create the book as it was meant to be. I don't know if any other editor could have made this possible; I am grateful that he and his team at HarperOne did.

Making this book a dream come true is my partnership with Emily McDowell—the kind anyone toiling away in obscurity visions about. She fiercely defended this work and enhanced it greatly with her clear-eyed thinking, relatable and witty writing, and artistic talent. We mind-melded seamlessly about what this book should be, she gave to it everything she had and more, and our collaboration has been one of the greatest professional experiences of my career.

With all the care that has gone into this work, none has been more important than that of my husband's, Mike Brown. His investment in me as a human, as his wife, and as an example to our daughter came before any other considerations. There is no conceivable way to describe the emotional, strategic, and financial support he provided to make me happy and the world a better place. He is more generous, patient, and funny than any man I know. I love him deeply.

This book is for my mother, who nurtured me until she no longer could, and for my husband, who nurtures me now and always will.

EMILY Says:

As it turns out, it takes a village to help you run a company while you're writing and illustrating a book. Big huge thanks to my employees, who picked up the slack like champions while I worked on this project. I'd also like to thank the fabulous folks who worked hard to help make this book happen: Myrsini Stephanides and Lydia Shamah at Carol Mann Agency, my superstar lawyer Marc Chamlin, and the whole team at HarperOne. To my partner, Seth: thank you for your infinite patience, saintlike willingness to listen to me complain, good ideas, and insistence that I'm pretty even when I'm definitely not. I owe you one. To my stepson, Oliver: thank you for being you. To Jenny: thank you for always showing up (then and now). To Amy O: thank you for living your life in a way that inspired me to make mine better. You are so missed. And, of course, to Kelsey: thank you for being a wonderful coauthor and friend. I am so happy and grateful to know you.

Finally, to all of the wonderful people who wrote about, shared, and bought Empathy Cards, and to everyone who shared their personal stories of illness and grief with me: thank you. This book is for you.

ABOUT THE AUTHORS

DR. KELSEY CROWE

Kelsey Crowe, Ph.D., founded Help Each Other Out and is a breast cancer survivor. She earned her doctorate in social welfare at the University of California, Berkeley, and teaches social work at California State University. Kelsey is originally from Brooklyn and lives in San Francisco with her husband and daughter. You can find her online at www.helpeachotherout.org.

EMILY McDOWELL

Emily McDowell is not a doctor. She is a writer, illustrator, speaker, and the CEO of Emily McDowell Studio, making greeting cards for the relationships we really have and products that speak to the people we really are. In

2015, she created Empathy™ Cards, for people experiencing major illness, grief, and loss. She and her work have been featured in the *New York Times* and on *Good Morning America*, *NBC Nightly News*, and NPR's *All Things Considered*, among many others, and in 2015, she was named by *Slate* as one of "Ten Designers Who Are Changing the World." Emily lives and works in Los Angeles, and you can find her online at www.emilymcdowell.com. This is her first book.